The Wildfowler

A Tale of the Shannon Estuary

On a good day the salt marshes of the Shannon Estuary would be black with birds – geese, snipe, teal, widgeon, woodcock, plover. . .

Armed with a puntgun, a cumbersome but deadly muzzle-loader with a barrel nine feet long, you could lift a hundred birds on one outing – a veritable hunter's paradise. Pad Moran, the wildfowler of the title, ranged these marshes with his dog, his guns and his young son – a free spirit on the edge of society. The author now recalls their expeditions together with a beguiling blend of lyricism and humour that belies the barbarity of their weaponry.

But *The Wildfowler* is more than a portrait of a hunter; almost imperceptibly it draws the reader into a world of apparently casual savagery, where the political upheavals of the young Irish State are expressed in electric violence, where a repressive religion reigns alongside ancient superstition, and a man's life is worth less than the animals he tends.

The result is a heady mixture of mayhem and murder, sadism and ignorance, buffoonery and backbiting, which, while it appears naturalistic, at the same time taps the dark forces of the primitive subconscious. The energy and power of his narrative place Moran firmly in the tradition of the *seanchaithe*, the storytellers who were the custodians of Ireland's ancestral lore.

A beautiful and original book destined to become a classic of Irish writing.

Roger Moran was 'bred, born and reared' in a labourer's cottage at New Quay, Askeaton, in the County of Limerick.

'We belonged to a group known in Ireland as "Cotteers", a derogatory term for the poor or working classes. From my childhood I pursued the packs of wild duck and geese on the Shannon and Deel Estuaries with a shooting punt and murderous muzzle-loader puntgun. I was "crewman" for my father Pad, who was the greatest wildfowler that ever lived.

'I have no formal education and in fact, because of our financial situation, departed our local "house of learning" in my thirteenth year, obliging my father to appear in the local district court to account for my absence. I loved that man with all my strength and with all my heart, and in my sorrow at his loss this book was born.'

The
WILDFOWLER

The WILDFOWLER

A Tale of the Shannon Estuary

ROGER MORAN

**illustrated by
Diana Oxlade**

The Blackstaff Press

British Library Cataloguing in Publication Data

Moran, Roger
  The wildfowler.
  1. Shannon, River (Ireland) – Description and travel
  I. Title
  914.17'047082   DA990.S/

  ISBN 0-85640-277-X
     0-85640-278-8 pbk

First published in 1982

© Roger Moran, 1982

Published by The Blackstaff Press Limited
3 Galway Park, Dundonald BT16 0AN
with the assistance of
The Arts Council of Northern Ireland

Printed in Northern Ireland by Universities Press Limited

"Fly will dive underwater after wounded water-hens...."

One

It's 'that' time of the month again for Old Rooney the Master. Six of us are standing in line before him. He's tossing an ashplant in his hand as he moves along the line of boys. He turns to me. 'What delayed you?' he asks. 'And make it good.' My mind is working overtime, I dare not give an excuse I've used before. 'I had to tie the Gandalo, sir,' I say. He looks at me from under bushy eyebrows. 'Had you now? I suppose we could say you were mooring the liner?'

He addresses the boy next to me. 'What about you, what were you tying?' 'Nothing, sir. I was up on Tom Charley's Hill looking for the ass, sir.' The Master puts his hands to his head. 'Jesus almighty,' he says, 'one ass looking for another ass.'

Near the end of the line, he nudges a little runt of a lad with the point of his stick. 'Snipe?' 'Yes, sir.' 'Have ye any apples down there this year?' The lad he referred to as 'Snipe' shrinks visibly into his clothes. 'No, sir,' he says, 'not an apple, they didn't grow at all.' The Master stoops and glares into Snipe's face. 'I'm not surprised,' he says. 'I suppose ye ate the blossoms off the trees!'

I wonder which end of the line he'll start using the stick. Why did I have to be late today of all days, it is drawing towards the end of the month and his cheque won't be here for a few days yet. We will continue to suffer his wrath as his raging porter thirst takes holt and burns abated.

Woe betide the boy that gets in his bad books during the next few days, until his money arrives and he can once more quench the fire raging within him.

Suddenly he swipes the stick across the shins of the boy nearest him; the lad jumps and howls with pain, and gets another lash on the backside for good measure. He's coming back up the line, dishing out

1

medicine left right and centre. We fall back in confusion, but there is no escape, and we go to our desks nursing our shins and backsides, wishing a speedy, and if possible painful, end to Old Rooney.

I believe he secretly enjoys himself when boys are late for school. It gives him an opportunity to show off his wit.

I share the desk with Jim Brody, he suffers from some type of brain-block. His parents run a small farm near our house, and they own a grey mare. Jim has a deep affection for this animal.

The previous week, the Master had given us a lesson on the history of the horse in Irish agriculture. He explained that when the animal was first used in Ireland, the farmers tied him to the plough by the tail.

He has the English book open now, he will question us on the lesson of last week.

'Brody?' 'Yes, sir?' 'Spell horse.' Jim is on his feet, he shuffles his books and looks up at the ceiling. 'You won't see it up there, Brody. I'll ask you once more, spell horse.' Jim wrings his hands and blurts out, 'H.O.R.S.E. horse grey mare!'

The Master walked to the window and stared out, for what seemed a long time; then he remarked over his shoulder, 'The morning you were born, your mother would have been better off if a jackdaw flew down the chimney.'

Before lunch, it's time for the sums. In this classroom must surely be the greatest selection of odd characters, apart altogether from Jim Brody. The fellow that was up on Tom Charley's Hill looking for the ass is brought to the blackboard and given a simple addition sum.

'Add three, four, and two.' No move from the boy. The Master tries another tack, he knows this boy's family keeps ferrets and spends a lot of time killing rabbits. 'Very well then,' the Master tells him, 'add three rabbits, four rabbits, and two rabbits.'

Without pausing, the lad replies, 'Nine rabbits, sir.'

The Master walks to the window again and stares out, then he mutters under his breath, 'I can see ye'll go a long way.'

At last the school day ends and I run as fast as I can towards home. Will he wait for me, I wonder. The Master had held us all back after school, just to make sure we'll know the difference between horses and mares in future. If Jim Brody was to get my prayers, he wouldn't have any more need of horses or mares.

I reach the house by the quay. Pad is out at the front, cleaning the great puntgun, thank God, he's not gone after all.

'What delayed you?' he asks.

'We were kept in,' I tell him.

2

'What did you do this time?' he wants to know.

'I didn't do anything,' I told him, 'it was Brody and his grey mare.' He looked at me oddly, but didn't pursue the matter.

'Come on,' he says, 'we'll have our dinner.' Our dinner was simple fare, a pot of spuds and plenty of goat's milk, it tastes just beautiful.

'Are you going to load the puntgun?' I ask him. 'We might as well,' he says. 'The geese are resorting the long mud, I heard them flying up from there this morning.' 'Will we load both barrels?' I ask. 'Hold on,' he says. 'Do you want to kill them all? If we got one shot at them we wouldn't be doing so bad.'

'Come on,' he says, 'you have enough spuds. There's no time for making buttons, it will soon be dark.'

We go out to the puntgun, it is a muzzle-loader and has two barrels, it is a murderous-looking weapon. He has just washed it out with boiling water. This is necessary to remove the soot left by the last shot. After washing, the gun must be placed near a fire and the flame drawn into the barrels to dry out your gun. A piece of oakum is twisted round the screw on the end of the ramrod and pulled back and forth through the barrel. This acts as the soaker on a pump, drawing in the flame with a whistling sound, and dries out the barrel.

This performance must also be carried out if the gun has been loaded for several days and will not fire. The problem here will be condensation, and the charge must be withdrawn from the barrel and the gun again washed out. If on occasion a charge must be withdrawn, great care must be taken to ascertain that all the gunpowder is removed.

Two winters previously, we were obliged to withdraw a charge from this weapon. The bronze measure was used to check that all the gunpowder was removed, but the careful attention that should have attended this operation was not adhered to, with almost tragic consequences. When it was believed that all the charge was drawn, the gun was again scalded and placed near the kitchen fire. The ramrod was then used in the usual fashion to draw the flame into the barrels. My father was standing at the mouth of the great gun, drawing the ramrod back and forth, when suddenly there was an almighty flash and roar. The ramrod shot up the sleeve of his coat and out at the elbow, passed through a bedroom door, rebounded off the wall and shot back through the door, though by now its force was spent. We will make sure to check the measurement of powder more carefully in future.

The puntgun will be loaded with coarse black powder. It is slow burning, and for this reason, the barrels of the gun are nine feet long.

This allows the charge to reach its full potential before reaching the muzzle. The nipples are filled with fine cartridge powder. This is a job for me, as you need perfect sight for this operation. The charge of powder is rammed tight with oakum, a type of hairy fibre. The loose grains of shot are held in place by a wad of paper. Pad has a little rhyme he sometimes recites to himself when he's doing this job:

> Ram your powder
> Not your lead;
> If you don't
> You won't kill dead.

The gun is fired by a percussion cap placed over the nipple. When this is struck by the hammer of the lock, the resulting flash through the nipple sets off the charge.

We're ready for off. The transporting of this gun is a problem. It is sixteen stone in weight. Most of this weight is concentrated at the breach where the charge is located, therefore I will take the lighter muzzle end.

We cross the field to the shore where the punt is moored. This punt is twenty-four feet long and four feet beam midships, tapering to a point fore and aft. The fore peak is decked and it is here the gun will be placed. The muzzle is placed on the rest, a piece of wood the shape of the letter 'M'. At the right top corner of the 'M' a bar is screwed through, and the end of this bar with ring attached reaches back into the punt. The breech rests on a huge metal spur which passes through the deck and fits into a steel plate secured to the bottom of the boat. Near the breach is a fitting we call the 'kicking bar'. This holds the breach rope. This rope passes through a hole in the stem of the punt under the muzzle of the great gun, both ends are drawn back and secured to the 'kicking bar'.

When the gun is fired, so great is the recoil that the boat is driven back several feet through the water, so it can be understood why it is important to have this rope in perfect condition and well secured. It has broken before with near tragic results.

We will also take a double-barrelled shoulder gun; we will need this to stop the 'cripplers' (wounded birds after a shot from the puntgun).

When all the gear is loaded in the punt and we get on board ourselves, there is just six inches of clear-board showing over water. I sit on a two-gallon drum and pull the two small oars. Pad is on the stern with the punting paddle. This is four feet long and is essential for this type of fowling.

We are going down-river fast, with the tail-end of a flood. A bunch of teal flashes over our heads going like lightning. Pad curls his nose at the fast-retreating teal and then looks towards the marshy ground to the west. 'I hope there are none of those poppers around, firing at the wind,' he said.

If it's one thing puntgunners cannot abide, it's poppers. This is the jargon for people shooting along the shore and on the marshes. It is indeed a frustrating situation, when you waste perhaps a full day setting up a good shot for the big gun at a pack of geese or duck, and have punted your boat for miles lying on your back, and when you're almost within range of your target, some popper on the shore fires a shot and scatters your ducks or geese to the four winds.

If the curses rained down on these poppers by puntgunners should fall on them, their term on this planet would indeed be short.

We're moving towards the creek leading into the area of the Long Mud. This shooting ground reaches from the north point of White Island, east to the little island of Lan Tighe and the Deel Estuary. I will now stow my oars and spurs, the oil drum will be pushed under the deck. Pad removes the shutter from the side of the punt near the stern. When he lies on his back and uses the little paddle his elbow will be only three inches from the water.

I pull the firing-hammer back to half-cock and remove the piece of oakum from the nipple. He hands me the percussion cap from a little bottle he carries in his pocket (a bottle is best to keep them dry). He sits on the bottom of the punt, I lie down facing forward. We haven't seen anything, but it doesn't pay to be caught napping. If you're making yourself conspicuous in a shooting punt and wild geese are anywhere in the vicinity, you can be sure those geese will have seen you and take to their heels.

Pad is punting west through the creek, the tide is helping him. Not so the wind, which is north-west. Well, you can't have it everyway. If the wind is blowing from behind you, it's good-night and safe home to the geese. They can smell you a mile off, and not necessarily because of BO.

Still no sign. Plenty curlew rising ahead of us, they're wary devils. We pass a drake teal standing on the slob all alone, his green and brown head resting on his wing: that must say something for the skill of the man doing the punting. The little duck completely ignores us. Then we round a turn in the creek: straight ahead, standing proudly on the mudbank, are about thirty barnacle geese. The watchman gander is standing higher than the rest, his neck fully extended. Here is the danger, is he high enough to see into the punt from his vantage point?

At the first sight of geese Pad has stretched himself full length on his back; nothing must now show above the outline of the punt. I creep my hand forward and pull back the firing-hammer to full-cock. Pad must now sight the gun. He will estimate the height of the geese and then aim the punt at a similar height, and instruct me if he requires the gun raised or lowered. This is a simple matter of using the rest holding up the gun on the deck. Pull back the rest and the gun elevates, push it forward and the gun lowers. Any movement to left or right must be performed by turning the boat.

We're ready to move forward. I'm trying to wriggle away from the breech as much as possible: the report from this weapon has a terrible effect on the head. I'm also wary of the hammers that fire it. On occasion it has blown them off. The trouble is, what direction do they take? There is ample evidence along the coaming of the punt where they have struck on their flight. It wouldn't be very nice if one should strike you on the head!

I have the piece of string from the trigger twisted round my fingers and held tight. The signal to pull is a sharp kick on the backside from the man punting. We're still moving towards the geese at a snail's pace; the temptation to raise your head and have a look is almost overpowering. I know I dare not do it if I value my life.

He's muttering something under his breath, 'The bastards of curlew will put them up.'

The gun is loaded with BB shot, this is best for geese, the grains are big and will carry far.

He's muttering and grunting again, trying to keep the punt moving against the breeze. What's he saying now? 'They'll put them up, I tell you.' Then he shouts at the top of his voice, 'They're getting up, let them have it!' and I pull the string.

The explosion almost bursts my brain. I get up on my knees and rock backwards and forwards, my ears are ringing. 'Watch the flock,' he shouts, 'watch the flock.'

Ahead of us on the mud six barnacle geese are dead; they seem a long shot. The flock is flying wildly towards the south-east. As they pass over Hayes's Marsh one seems to stagger in mid-air, then drop like a stone to the ground. 'Hah,' he says. 'I thought he was sick. We'll get him later.'

We paddle up to where the six geese are lying quietly, I get out and pick them up. They seem in good condition. Sometimes wild geese can be thin and scraggy and tough as an old boot.

'They were too far from us,' Pad remarks. 'Those bloody curlew, there's nothing a match for them. It's not the first time they blackguarded me.'

'We didn't do too bad,' I say. 'Six here and one over on the marsh, it could have been worse.'

We paddle back out the creek towards Hayes's Marsh and our seventh goose. This marsh is criss-crossed with trenches, some ten feet deep and usually filled with water. We paddle in along one of these and try to locate our goose. The light is fading fast now and it will soon be dark. We must be near him. I get out on the marsh and begin hopping over the trenches this way and that trying to spot him.

A barnacle goose is striped and is therefore partially camouflaged in these surroundings. Then I see him near a clump of rice grass. He seems to be sitting quietly and is probably dead.

I run towards him to pick him up. When I'm almost placing my hand on his back he jumps up and takes off running like the hammers of hell. I'm close on his heels: I'm barefooted and this gives me an advantage.

The gap between us is closing fast; I jump across a porteen to grab him and find myself struggling up to my neck in water and mud.

The goose has changed direction and is now racing hard for the tide, but he's made a serious mistake, he's fast bringing himself within range of the man in the punt who is now standing up holding the shoulder gun. Suddenly there is a shot and the goose turns somersault and lays still.

I drag myself out of the trench, covered with slime and wet through. As I'm climbing onto solid ground, I hear him say, 'Any place there will do you.' If you get wet around here you needn't expect any sympathy. I pick up the seventh goose and get back in the punt. I can see Pad smirking behind his hand. I suppose if he had fallen in, I'd laugh too. We pull away for home.

If you examine those cookbooks that provide recipes for the cooking of wild geese, they will tell you to hang the bird for at least a week with some onions pushed into his craw and other herbs stuffed up his backside. This, they say, will make him tender and flavoursome. If any members of my family should read those recipes it would give them something to laugh at. If a wild goose is very old you can hang him for a month of Sundays and he won't get tender, he will probably rot and you will find yourself eating carrion instead of a corpse.

When we reach home and place the seven geese on the kitchen floor, the mother examines them and sorts them out. She picks out what she believes are the best two for our own table; the small ones will be sold at five shillings each.

The three-legged pot is already hanging on the pothooks over the fire and the feathers are being pulled off a goose as fast as the mother can

7

manage it. When the bulk of the feathers are off, the bird is held by the neck over the fire and the remainder are singed off. Draw out the guts (all disgarded except the gizzard), rinse with a sup of water and the goose is in the pot over the fire boiling merrily. A pinch of salt and a couple of onions completes the flavouring. We all hope it will be tender enough for us to eat it; last week we boiled one for hours: the longer it remained on the fire the tougher it became. My mother had poked it with a fork a few times and I heard her remark under her breath, 'You're as hard as a whore's heart.'

Tonight we're in luck, this is a fine young bird and very soon shows signs of cooking. The only meat that comes into this house is supplied by the gun. Often, many days pass with just the 'crockauns' and milk, so now we're all looking forward to this feast. The only danger is the soup, it has a devastating effect on the bowels. A glutton could pay dearly if he was tempted to indulge himself, as I know to my cost.

We must make preparations for next morning, the geese are also resorting an area south of Holly Island on Hewson's Marsh. We will come on them here from the land if that is possible. The grass in this area seems to hold a great attraction for them.

Pad has loaded special cartridges for this operation; extra powder is added; the wads holding the shot are disgarded; he will put in bigger grains he has made himself by rolling melted lead in a pot. The grains are held in position with candlegrease.

I will use a sixteen-bore muzzle-loader we have had in the family for generations. Its appearance is deceptive. One might think it small and frail, it is in fact a deadly killer. The only trouble with it is, it has a kick like a wicked jennet.

We have a fantastic gun dog. He will dive underwater after wounded duck; point snipe, woodcock, pheasants, water hens or indeed any type of game. He is a bastard greyhound. In his time he has flabbergasted shooters that have come to this area. Some of these characters had gone so far as to have their very expensive gun dogs sent to Scotland to 'reputable' trainers to have them 'schooled'. They would smile behind their aristocratic hands at the sight of this humpy-looking article hopping along behind us. Their smiles were short-lived however, when he went to work and left their expensive parlour dogs floundering in his wake. He has of course, 'just like the rest of us', his faults; he is a disobedient beggar.

Dawn next morning finds Pad and me, closely followed by Fly, 'an apt name', crawling on hands and knees towards the tidal bank of

"When the bulk of feathers are off, the bird is held by the neck over the fire ....."

Hewson's Marsh. The geese are giving tongue as they always do at this time of morning when they are preparing for their flight inland. We have no way of knowing if they are within range of the bank, but the tide is full and more than likely they are feeding on the grass at the water's edge. If this is so, then may the God of geese help them. The sound of goose music is getting too much for Fly and he's whimpering and talking to himself. Suddenly he flashes past us and goes over the bank like a rocket, into the midst of the geese. As he went over the top, Pad called him a name which should have turned him then and there to ashes.

My God, it's too much. We've been crawling for over an hour through briers and bushes to reach this spot and now this. Pad is sitting back on heels shaking his head from side to side as if he cannot believe his luck; his jaws are working but no sound comes out. But there is also something strange going on outside the bank. When Fly shot over the top there was a wild flurry of wings and screeching of geese taking off, and then the sound of hundreds of bodies striking the water. The geese it seems have not flown away, merely rushed into the tide. Pad looks at me and signals to follow him and begins again to crawl towards the bank. He turns the peak of his cap to the back, and moves slowly and carefully to the top where he peeps through a tuft of grass, then ducks his head back as if he can't believe his eyes. He signals me to have a peep, and I also look through the grass. Fly is sitting on his backside at the water's edge surrounded by dozens of wild geese, happily wagging his tail and daring them to come closer. The geese for their part are swimming up and down and look as if they might peck out his eyes at any moment.

Pad gives me a nudge. 'I'll count to three. Aim for their heads,' he says under his breath. 'One, two, three, up guns, let them have it.'

If ever a flock of geese got a surprise it was those. When the smoke cleared, five of them were lying dead on the water and Fly was retrieving them to the shore, his recent crime forgotten in the flush of success.

We move for home as fast as we can, I have to go to school and face Old Rooney the Master and it now looks as if I'll be late again today. I have one chance, I will bring him one of the geese. He will pay the going price of five shillings, that is, when his cheque arrives and I can put the bite on him when he changes it in Jack Foley's pub. That publican is also a customer for a goose. I will take a few of them in a sack when going to school and sell them in the afternoon. The master has a great liking for all types of game. He also likes apple cakes, and a few cooking apples in the school-bag saved many a boy from a cut of the ashplant on the backside when he found himself late in the mornings.

I'll run the two miles to the school as fast as I can. I have the sack, with four geese tucked in the bottom. It has seen a lot of service: numerous feathers are sticking to it, also many stains of dried blood.

I enter the schoolroom; he's just about to call the rolls. 'My, my,' he says. 'Look who's coming now. The Wildfowler.'

Two

I watch him from the corner of my eye, he doesn't seem to be making any move to go for the ashplant and I slip in beside Jim Brody.

Some years previously during the War of Independence when the holding of firearms was punishable by death, Pad had given Old Rooney a bad fright on the village bridge which spans the River Deel.

Pad had hidden most of his guns. Some were buried in the ground, more hidden in haybarns, but one breech-loader he could not bring himself to put away. He made himself a harness to carry the gun on his person. This harness fitted round his shoulders and ended in a hook under his right armpit. A ring screwed into the stock and placed over this hook, and the gun would be carried under the coat without arousing any suspicion.

Old Rooney was standing on the bridge at nightfall, watching two otters chasing a salmon. These clever little animals have the natural hunting instinct. One would cut off the fish's escape down-river and turn it back towards its companion; the other would attempt to prevent it going under the arches of the bridge and making its escape up-river. The old schoolmaster was fascinated; he hopped and jumped with excitement and clapped his hands. Pad came walking along the green towards the bridge, and when Rooney sighted him he shouted, 'Quick, Pad, quick, look at this.'

Pad moved behind him and then, unseen by Rooney, slipped the gun from under his coat, pushed two cartridges into the barrels and in an instant discharged left and right at the two otters.

For a moment Old Rooney was stunned, then he grabbed his hat from his head and bolted for the green as fast as his legs would carry him. To say he was frightened would be to understate the situation, he was literally running for his life. Pad was close on his heels and perhaps was only now beginning to realise the folly of the act he had just performed. They made their escape through the fields north of the village, just in time. The bridge where the shots were fired was less than one hundred yards from the barrack and in minutes the street was bristling with 'Tans' and military in search of the ambush party.

Old Rooney would give Pad a wide berth for many a day after this incident.

The rolls are over and it's time for sums again. Today he will lay out a few problems on the blackboard.

Jim Brody gives me a tip with his leg under the desk and then slips me a piece of paper. 'Write a few answers on that and I'll bring you four Woodbines tomorrow,' he whispers behind his hand. Four Woodbines was indeed big payment for such a small amount of work. It was terrific to get permission from the Master to go to the hole at the back of the school we called the 'lav' and sit on the plank over this pit and puff away at your fag. It also helped to kill the foul smell coming from the mountain of decaying mixtures that lay therein. Beyond the wall dividing our school from the Girls was another hole topped by a similar plank and which we could only assume smelled as bad as our own.

He's coming around checking the answers against those on the board; soon he arrives behind myself and Jim Brody. A school-master standing behind your back surveying your work and not making a sound in the process has a terrible effect on the mind, when you don't know if you're going to get a thump on the pole or not.

Finally he remarks in a quiet voice, which doesn't bode well for someone. 'Where did you get those answers, Jim?' Jim fidgets on his seat and begins to turn pale, then he says, 'In my head, sir.' A clout on the ear starts Jim bawling. 'Where did you get those answers?' The master asks him again. 'In my head, sir.' A much harder clout on the other ear really gets poor Jim in a state, and as the Master raises his hand to make another strike, Jim's resistance is gone and he points at me. 'From him, sir.'

Old Rooney is white with rage. 'Ahah, the wildfowler again. Bend over the desk and take your medicine.' 'I won't, I didn't do anything. He must have copied them from me without I knowing.' 'Is that a fact? And what were you writing on the piece of paper he slipped you under the desk? Bend over, I said, and no more of your tricks. I'll warm you now.'

In the ensuing struggle, with Rooney trying to get me over the desk and I doing my best to prevent him, he has to be satisfied with the few swipes he gets at my shins. 'I'll complain you to your father and that's the boy to give you what's coming to you,' he shouts, then he goes back to the top of the class white in the face and shaking.

I'm rubbing my legs where the stick has connected and giving sour looks at Brody. What else could I expect from him, with his H.O.R.S.E., horse-grey-mare. The fact that the Master had us under observation during our clandestine dealings I just could not accept.

Jim Brody belonged to a strange family. They suffered from what might be called 'baby-ism'! There is nothing a baby likes better than to pull off its clothes and romp about in the nude. The Brodys had brought this trait with them into adult life, and were to be seen frequently cavorting in the fields in their pelt. The previous winter I had come upon a male member of the family, quite naked, tumbling somersaults in the corner of a field, his clothes thrown in a heap nearby.

Their farm was situated close to my own house and I often passed that area with my father during the hours of darkness on our way to and from the shore in the pursuit of wildfowl. One bitterly cold January morning, stalking a hedgerow in search of the early cock pheasant, my father suddenly stopped in his tracks and, signalling me to join him, pointed ahead with a look of utter disbelief on his face, to where a huge woman was performing weird acrobatics on the pier of a gate, naked as a scalder. On closer scrutiny, unobserved, we discovered one of the Brody females performing a fan dance without the fans.

Sometimes when we passed by their house late at night, we heard the sound of great weeping coming from within, as if some terrible sorrow sat on the souls of the people inside. At these times I moved closer to Pad and gripped tighter on my muzzle-loader; it seemed somehow to give me comfort.

Jim Brody was an only child. His father was unique: in a family of twenty-two, he was the only one to marry. Of these twenty-two only seven now remain, the rest are gone to their eternal reward. They were all of immense physique, yet they died off like flies in the space of a few years. The family burial plot was at Lis Ma Keera churchyard, and so fast were the members of the family going into the earth there that on the advice of a 'hob lawyer' they were persuaded that the burial ground was jinxed and a new plot should be acquired in a neighbouring parish. However, the jinx, if jinx it was, was not impressed by this attempt to outmanoeuvre it, and the brown boxes continued to come out of the boreen leading from the Brody household.

At last it's lunch-time and we get into the fresh air. We climb over the stile leading to Tom Charley's Hill. Why it is called a hill I'll never

14

know, there isn't any hill that I can see nearer than six miles. However it is here we have our skeets. These are well-worn paths on a sloping area of the field, the steeper the slope the better. We will wet these paths, most times with our urine, and then running back some distance, and with a wild yell of childish delight, run as fast as we can, jump onto the skeet and slide its full length on our bare feet.

Those wearing boots are barred from this game. The boot breaks the nice smooth surface of the skeet, made with the bare feet. We didn't have to bar many, most of the boys were bare of foot.

Children can be unbelievably cruel to each other, and why not? After all, they are tomorrow's adults. Most boys have nicknames, some of these are quite outlandish. One chap, he was one of those few to have a fine pair of hobnailed boots which were known at the time as 'farmers' friends', had the unusual name of Tom Saucepan.

All nicknames were pertinent, and Tom Saucepan's was no exception. It would be said that his mother was a fantastic exponent of the art of pishoguery. To perform this powerful magic she had a special saucepan. When the time came to launch the attack on her chosen victim, she would move into the fields at the dead of night when she was to be seen walking backwards and forwards, at the same time holding the saucepan at arm's length, the open end towards the ground. Once this black rite was completed, the crops were to be seen visibly wilting.

It is an authenticated fact that throughout the area of West Limerick and North Kerry farmers were destroyed by what they believed was the work of pishoguery. To try and put forward the argument that this was a natural phenomenon, was futile. Farmers brought in priests, missioners, and even monks, reputed to have the power to cope with this evil.

Belief in pishoguery was rooted deep in the Irish countryside. There were many systems besides walking the fields with a saucepan. You could also use eggs or fat bacon, but, the most important factor of all, you needed a close relationship with the Prince of Darkness. For some reason, men did not seem to fit into the required mould to perform these rites. One might be forgiven for the thought that Old Nick was, or is, strictly heterosexual!

Eggs were mostly used to remove potatoes and other root crops from gardens. The eggs were planted in the freshly-turned drills shortly after the victim had planted the seed. Fat bacon was buried in gardens of corn, eggs would not suffice here. The idea of all this being to remove the crop from the victim's land to that of the perpetrator, no mean feat if it could be pulled off.

What I found strange about all this, any time I had a glimpse of Tom Saucepan having his lunch, he was eating a chunk of dry bread just like myself. Surprising his mother, Maggie Saucepan, would not give him a piece of that bacon or some of those eggs she was supposed to have in such plentiful supply.

Tom took a poor view of his nickname, so much so that he was inclined to draw a lash with his 'farmers' friends' across the shin bone of any boy he could lay hands on during these playground exchanges. I was very wary of Tom Saucepan. I would never dream of calling him that dreadful name, not because his nail boots might connect with my shin bone, but supposing he was to borrow his mother's deadly container some morning and fetch it to school, who knows what mischief he might wreak with same. 'It doesn't cost anything to be careful!'

Maggie had the ability to make pregnant cows abort their calves. She would creep into cow byres in the dead of night and draw milk from the springing udders. Sprinkling the milk over the stalled animals she recited her weird prayer to Satan. Soon, most of these cows would loose their calves. In later years, modern-thinking vets would have us believe this was caused by a disease with a high-faluting name, 'brucellosis'. We of course could tell them the real cause.

The fact that I refrained from calling Tom names meant he in turn developed an attachment to me. He even took to inviting me to visit his home during weekends. At first I treated these invitations with caution, but my curiosity overcame my fear and I took the plunge. The family lived across the river from us, and it was a simple matter to cross over in the boat and walk through some fields to reach the house.

As I approached, Maggie was working in her garden. She was dressed all in black and had a terrible stoop in her back. The fact that she wore black might be misconstrued as indicating that she was a widow. This was not the case. It would have been a happy release for her if she was. She was married to a good-for-nothing drunkard that spent his days slugging porter in the black smelly holes of the village that passed for public houses. Here he spent the few hard-earned shillings she made selling vegetables from door to door on her donkey and cart. People bought them more from fear than necessity; most times the vegetables were dumped or burned when her back was turned.

She had a magnificent orchard of cooking apples – the blossoms weren't eaten off the trees here! After I'd become a regular caller, many a huge chunk of beautiful apple cake I devoured, washed down with a fine mug of strong tea, sitting at the end of her kitchen table.

16

Without question she was a bitter old woman, and who could blame her? For years she was ostracised by malicious gossip and scandal-mongering. A short while before I first entered her house, the clergy were obliged by 'outraged public opinion' to visit her house and sort her out. One could not blame the clergy, I suppose. They were victims of the same environment as the rest of us.

The day of their visit had not been a good one for Maggie, by any means. Her spouse had returned early from the village, having been unable to beg, borrow or tick any more porter. This of course was Maggie's fault. What became of all the money she made from the vegetables? Hadn't he come to a sorry lot when he hadn't the price of a pint? After two hours of his scurrilous tirade, he took himself to his bed to recharge his batteries. Maggie felt like tears, but she had discovered long ago it was a futile business.

Into the midst of her misery strode the avengers, the Parish Priest and curate. They didn't beat about the bush; they had come to order her once and for all to desist from these awesome satanic rites before a terrible curse fell on her.

It was the last straw for a woman that was tired from taking beatings from life. She rounded on the two clergy like a tigress. 'Clear out of here, ye pair of bastards,' she shouted, 'or I'll give ye this.' 'This' was a well-seasoned ashplant she had taken from beside the fire, and was now warping the boards on the kitchen table with savage swipes of the same plant.

The elder priest at first tried the soft approach, and said if she would vow on her knees to abandon her evil ways, he was prepared to be lenient; if not, he would be left with no choice but to use his own terrible powers, and very probably she would find herself turned into a goat.

He was not however in a position to deliver this threat; what he did succeed in doing was preventing that hard-working woman from ever again going to Mass or the Sacraments.

On her last day in the Chapel, it was clearly seen that the moment she opened her bag a mouse jumped out and ran pell-mell for the front door of the church. As it was running it began to grow in size, and with its huge teeth bared, began snapping at the shins and heels of those people seated nearest the centre aisle. It was only by a miracle, and the fact that the front door was open to allow its escape, that the creature did not wreak untold havoc on the assembled throng . . . Ireland and your children – you have a lot to answer for.

The land adjoining Tom Saucepan's house was a game preserve.

While he was showing me round his mother's garden one afternoon, he pointed away across the broad fields. 'Can you see that grove of trees over there?' he said. 'That place is full of pheasants; I can see them every morning and evening picking in the field.'

'A fat lot of good that is,' I told him. 'If you should get caught in there you'd get the darrig.' 'It could be done all right,' he said. 'The fellow that looks after them goes to First Mass in the village every Sunday morning.' 'Are you quite sure of that?' I said. 'Of course I'm sure,' he told me. 'He passes by the gate there on his way to and from the village.'

That night while we're cleaning the shotgun I relate my story to Pad. He chews his bottom lip and stares at me from under his bushy eyebrows. 'Do you want to draw the Shadogues down on us?' he said. 'Be careful of yourself, and never mind your harebrained notions.'

But I can see I have planted the seeds in his head. A few times that night, and then the next day I overheard him muttering and talking to himself. The following afternoon he calls me aside. 'Is that young fellow sure of his facts?' he asks. 'Of course he is,' I tell him.

'I don't know all about this course,' he says, 'but anyhow I'm game to give it a rub on Sunday morning.'

My heart bounds with excitement, but I make no comment.

Sunday morning finds us moving carefully along hedges and ditches leading to the Grove of the Pheasants. We have crossed the river by boat and are now drawing near our destination. We enter the field near the grove and look around carefully. No sign of life. Pad has a piece of strong twine around the neck of Fly and is keeping a firm grip on this with his right hand. We don't want him running away and causing more trouble.

Suddenly Fly comes to attention and cocks his ears. At the same instant a hen pheasant jumps up from the grass and runs into the grove of trees. Pad removes the string from the hound's neck, and man and dog begin to run towards the opposite side of the grove. Over his shoulder he says, 'You stay here and watch this side.'

A hen pheasant comes running fast out of the wood. A blast from the muzzle-loader tumbles her over, I pop her into a huge pocket inside my coat, and immediately set about reloading my gun.

First powder horn. Put finger over nipple at top of horn, turn horn upside down to fill measure, pour powder into gun, pull ramrod from rings under barrel and push piece of oakum down after powder. The charge of shot is already made up in a 'tosheen' and this is dropped into the barrel and held in place with a piece of paper. A few grains of

18

powder in the nipple for a primer, push a percussion cap over the nipple, pull back the lock hammer and you're ready to fire again, a lot faster than you might think.

Fly is barking in amongst the trees, and then I hear two shots from the other side. A flurry of wings over my head makes me look up. A huge cock pheasant comes streaking out of the trees going like a rocket, I point the gun and pull the trigger, the cock hits the ground in a cloud of feathers.

He's not dead however, and he's up and running, dragging a wing. A cock pheasant can run fast when he wants to, and this one wants to real bad. I'm soon close on his heels however, and he hasn't any place to hide. I have one fear, that Fly will come running out of the trees and get to the pheasant first. He has a very hard mouth and should he win the race, he would probably make mince of my bird.

When I get close enough to grab him, the cock does an about-turn and makes off in a different direction. I soon think of a plan for this, and when next I close with him I stand on his back and pin him to the ground. I bend and grab him by the head; he sets up a great flapping with his good wing and attempts to claw me with his feet.

As I'm trying to wring his neck, a bellow sounds behind me like a bull locked out of a field from a sexy cow, and turning I see a huge man holding his cap in his hand bearing down on me as fast as his legs would carry him. He is shouting again at the top of his voice. 'Stand, McDonnell you bastard, I know you.'

Whoever McDonnell the bastard was, it certainly wasn't me, but I had no intention of waiting to explain that to this roaring giant, and I took off across the field as fast as I could go.

The field in which I find myself running is comprised of perhaps twenty acres, and the boundary fence seems a long way off. I'm not gaining an inch on my pursuer; if anything the gap between us is closing.

At last I reach the boundary, which is a grass bank topped by strands of barbed wire plus a growth of furze and briers. I bound to the top, to be faced with a wide trench at the other side. I have no choice, and I spring onto the next field.

The jolt when I hit the ground almost dislocated my hip joints. I pitched forward, still trying to save my beloved muzzle-loader, and struck the ground a teeth-rattling blow with my forehead.

I'm up again and running along this ditch. My pursuer has crossed the ditch fifty yards to the south in what I believe is a move to cut me off, and he's now pounding along behind, calling on me to halt.

" He goes over the bank like a rocket, into the midst of the geese ...."

At the end of this field runs a railway track. If I could get onto this track I might yet make my escape. The bank here is well fenced, and I turn west along it, watching for a likely place to get over. At last I see a gap and rush through it; I gain the railway and hare away to the west.

My pursuer has had enough, he gets out onto the railway and looks after me. I can hear his voice growing fainter on the wind, 'I'll get you yet, McDonnell, you bastard.'

I make a wide detour back to the shore where we had left the boat. Pad is sitting on the stern smoking his pipe and talking to himself. He looked up and saw me. I noticed the tails of two pheasants hanging under his coat.

'What delayed you?' he asked with a sly grin.

'I took a walk,' I said. 'For the fresh air, like.'

'The last time I saw you,' he said, 'you were walking fairly lively.'

'In the name of God,' I asked him, 'who was that fellow?'

'That's the fellow that goes to First Mass every Sunday morning according to your friend Tom Saucepan.'

'How do you mean?' I said.

'What I mean is this,' he replied, 'you've just been chased by Old Budge Madigan the keeper.'

'He can't be that old,' I said. 'Did you see the way he could run?'

My father looked at me, his eyes dancing with devilment. 'Do you know something,' he laughed, 'you're fairly lively on the kippens yourself.'

Three

Our lunch break is over. We must abandon our skeets on Tom Charley's Hill and again face Old Rooney. He's out in the school yard ringing the bell, and we file past him into our school prison, for as such we thought of it. As I'm going by he grabs my shoulder and says, 'Don't forget, I'm still going to complain to your father.' I hold my peace; my shins are still sore since this morning.

During the lunch break he has been at my goose bag, and removed what he thinks is the best bird of the four, and dispatched one of the boys to his home in the village to deliver it to his daughter. He is a widower.

Seated at a desk before me is a fat boy named John Mahon. His house is famous, or infamous, depending on your point of view, for gambling and card-playing, and this goes on until all hours of the night, which means Mahon gets very little sleep.

I can see him now, nodding and dozing, his body weaving from side to side. It will be too bad if Old Rooney catches sight of him. All Mahon's family have been sea-going people. His grandfather was a ship's captain, and was lost when his ship foundered off Loop Head with the loss of all hands. His father is presently at sea serving as first mate on a cargo vessel.

Suddenly, Old Rooney gives a shout from the top of the room, 'MAHON, wake up you scamp and come up here at once.' No move from Mahon. He's still bobbing and weaving on the seat before me.

Rooney makes a rush from the top of the room and grabs Mahon by the scruff of the neck and drags him to the top of the class. He's wide awake now and that's for sure.

Old Rooney had long since grown tired of inflicting physical pain on John, he had never succeeded in making him cry, and he took this as a personal affront. He had however hit on a much more cruel method of punishment. 'Will ye all take a good look at him, the smart fellow. You are a smart fellow, aren't you, Mahon?' John stuck out his square stubborn chin. 'No, sir,' he said. 'Oh come now, don't be modest, Mahon, we all know you're a clever fellow. What are you going to be when you leave school?' John's chin seems to jut out still further. 'I don't know, sir,' he said.

Old Rooney is enjoying himself. 'Oh there's no doubt about it,' he says. 'You'll be a sailor. And I'll tell you something else, you'll make a good sailor, and do you know why?' John is showing signs of distress. 'No, sir,' he said. Old Rooney leans down and peers into the boy's face, then he shouts, 'You've a timber head and you'll never sink.' With that he gave John a dunt and sent him reeling back towards his seat. He won't fall asleep any more today.

After school I retrieve my goose bag and walk the short distance to the village.

I have three customers for the remaining geese. My last call is Jack Foley's pub. I push in the swing door leading form the street. The interior is dark after the sunlight; there is no sign of Jack. I go through the door leading to the kitchen at the back of the house. Jack is sitting on a sugain chair gazing into the fire. He doesn't raise his head or give any response to my rattling of the door handle. I go up to him and touch his shoulder, and he sits up and takes notice of me for the first time.

Jack Foley is under sentence of death. The black angel has been hovering over him for a long time now, but just recently the angry red lump on his neck is getting more noticeable over his shirt collar and it looks as if the sentence will very shortly be carried out. Jack Foley has cancer of the throat.

Jack's sentence was delivered in the form of a blow from an Irish Freedom Fighter. Jack is a bachelor, and perhaps because of this had gathered about himself a notorious pack of Tongavauns. These ne'er-do-wells would gather nightly in the kitchen behind the bar of his public house. Around the fireplace in that room was plotted most of the mischief carried out in the village and surrounding area.

During the War of Independence, a fellow publican at the eastern end of the village was the proud owner of two magnificent pigs. They should long since have been visited by the pork butcher, but so attached had the publican become to his porkers that he could not bring himself, as he put it, 'to do 'em in'.

Most days of the week when he took his constitutional walk after

23

dinner, from one end of the village to the other, he was accompanied by his two pigs. They walked one on either side of him like well-trained dogs. This man had come from an area north of the village, known as the Lough, and so he was soon given the nickname, Jim the Lough. Now, however, some wits of the village were inclined to refer to him as Jim the Hog.

At Jack Foley's fireside one winter's night, probably well lubricated with porter, sat the group of Tongavauns, sitting amongst them was Pad. The conversation turned to Jim the Lough and his pigs. 'He was back the street with them again today,' Jack told them.

In the group was a pair of twins. One of these was of a peaceful disposition, the other was a walking devil. 'Christ,' said the devil twin, 'Wouldn't it be great gas to steal them, and hide them somewhere for a few days?'

Some of the group agreed; others thought it just another harebrained scheme that this character seemed to produce with monotonous regularity. The decision for Pad was taken out of his hands. His wife knocked at the side door and asked him to come home. She was heavily pregnant with her second child, and was anxious to get home to bed. He left quietly in her company.

Shortly afterwards the devilish twin also slipped out the side door. Jack left the kitchen on a scouting mission. This entailed going to a small window in the gable-end of the house, and having a careful peep along the street to check on the movements of any policemen that just might take the notion to go raiding public houses. Jack surveyed the street slowly. Suddenly, across the bridge came a sight that made his eyes pop. The devilish twin was riding one of Jim the Lough's pigs, and chasing the other one before him.

The group of Tongavauns emerged from the side door onto the street, and soon the two porkers were rounded into a nearby yard where they were supposed to remain hidden for a few days until the hullabaloo died down, and then they would once more reappear in their sty, just as mysteriously as they had disappeared.

The incident started as innocent as that.

Before it would end, it unleashed such a volume of violence and bitterness as had not been seen in that village.

Sinn Fein were at that time beginning to form their own courts of law. Some of these were quite adequate, others left much to be desired. The enforcement arm of these courts was the Freedom Fighters. It is said that revolution makes for strange bedfellows; certainly there were some

24

beauties in the IRA organisation of the area. The Duke of Wellington once said the British Army was comprised of the scum of the earth. If that was, or is, true, I leave to History to judge, I am not qualified to do so. I am not so handicapped in the qualifications of some of our so-called Freedom Fighters.

The streets of our village were littered with drunken Black and Tans and Auxiliaries, lying on the footpaths, sleeping off their drunken binges, their weapons thrown on the ground beside them, and yet not a finger was raised in the locality against them. When word got out that Jim the Lough's pigs were missing, the Special Branch of the village went into action. Jim the Lough looked kindly on Sinn Fein. He also had a private room in his house where English officers could drink their whiskey in peace and privacy. A blind eye was turned to this – after all, business is business.

It was soon discovered that Jack Foley's Tongavauns had a hand in the disappearing pigs. It didn't take long to ferret out the names of the group that took part in it.

The first house to be visited by the 'Law-Enforcing Officers' was that of the peaceful twin. He was dragged from his bed in the middle of the night and kicked unconscious, then thrown into a waiting car. His wife, when she tried to intervene, was knocked to the ground, screaming from a kick in the stomach.

Next stop, Jack Foley's. The back door was burst in and six of the group rushed the stairway. The noise had awakened Jack and he ran onto the landing. The first of the group on the stairs was sent reeling back into the arms of his companions from a puck on the gob. They gathered themselves again and rushed him. Two were armed with rifles. Jack fought like a tiger, but he was soon overpowered. The one that had received the punch on the mouth snatched a rifle from a companion and crashed it down on Foley's neck. He was taken unconscious and dumped in the car with the twin.

Through the night the round-up went on. The only one to escape the dragnet was the devil twin.

At ten o'clock the next mornng, Pad was lying on the bed from the effects of a flu he had been fighting for several days. He was running a fever and, being a bad patient at the best of times, was feeling very sorry for himself. His wife was busily making up a witch's brew she believed was the very thing to deliver the death blow to this malady. A knock sounded at the door, and she went to open it. She found a little man quite well known to her standing there. His name was David O'Brien.

'God save you, missus, and how are you keeping?'

'Can't complain, David. What's troubling you this hour of the morning?'

This 'gentleman' had been to our house on several occasions – he had a liking for wildfowling. He was also a camp follower of the IRA. They tolerated him for one reason: he was small and slight of stature, and because of this he was very useful getting through the small windows of country houses and stealing whatever he could find – food, clothing, money, anything that might be of use to that organisation.

'Is Pad in?' he asked.

'Yes,' she tells him, 'but he's in bed with the flu, but I'm going to give him a dose now that will soon put him hopping out of it.'

'Tell him come out a minute, I want him,' he said.

'What do you want him for?' she asked suspiciously.

'There's a few of the boys out here, and we want the loan of a boat to put them across the Shannon to Clare. They're on the run,' he told her.

She went to the room and related the story to Pad. 'Tell him I can't go,' he said. 'The boat is over on the strand and they can work away themselves.'

She's back at the door. 'No good,' O'Brien tells her. 'We wouldn't know what boat to take. Tell him come out, it won't take a minute.'

Finally Pad got out of bed and walked on his stockinged feet to the front door.

'Good morrow, Dave.'

'Hello, Pad. You're not too good, I believe? The missus told me you have the flu. We want a boat, Pad. Will you be able to fix us up?'

'No problem, Dave, but ye'll have to go yerselves, I'm not up to it.'

'Alright,' said the little man. 'Come out to the gate 'til you meet a few of these fellows, they are anxious to see you.'

As they were talking, Pad started walking towards the front gate with David O'Brien. He hadn't yet seen any of those that required the boat. He stepped through the gateway onto the road and was immediately pounced on by two groups of men that had been hiding under the wall.

When Pad and his 'friend' left the front door for their walk to the gate, his wife returned to her interrupted job of putting together her cure-all. Suddenly a shout from the road brings her up short. It was Pad's voice. 'Mag, bring me out my guns.' She rushed to the door and out the passage leading to the roadway. She was in time to see a group of men, Pad amongst them, crashing in a lump against the boundary limestone wall at the front of the gate.

'Go back,' he shouted at her. 'Get my guns and release Merr.'

Merr was a Kerry Blue terrier bitch that was constantly chained to an alder tree near the door – for good reason – she was a savage hound. She was now going berserk and frothing at the mouth, as she heard her master's raised voice calling her name, and knew he was in trouble. She was making valiant efforts to gain her freedom and go to his assistance.

Mag ran back towards the door as fast as her pregnant state would allow. As she was slipping the chain from Merr's neck, O'Brien ran past her into the house. Merr tore onto the road. Nine men were hanging off various parts of Pad, trying to force him to the ground. He would wrench an arm free and crash his fist into the nearest face.

Merr sized up the situation at once, and sprang at the nearest buttocks. A Kerry Blue has a mouth and teeth unlike any other dog. They have a cluster of fangs at the front of their mouths, and when these lock in the closed position, getting them open again could be a difficult operation. Merr now locked her teeth on the buttocks of her choice and sprang backwards, carrying a mouthful of flesh and most of a pair of trousers. As she shook herself free of debris and prepared to spring again, two blasts from a shotgun at close range took off her head and scattered it in pieces about the roadway.

May the sod rest lightly on her grave.

Pad was shattered. He turned his head to look at his beloved dog, whose lifeless blood-spattered body lay on the grass margin.

The hyena, those animals accursed by God, and forced by their deformed bodies to live off carrion and the leavings of hunting animals, nevertheless will form themselves into packs and kill the king of beasts, should they find him wounded, unable to defend himself. So too will certain humans. When Pad turned his head to look at his dog, one of the group raised his rifle and brought the brass-shod butt down across his face with all his strength. The blow laid his face open to the bone, the wound reached from the corner of his right eye across his nose and down to the side of his mouth. He fell to the ground pouring blood.

When David O'Brien ran into the kitchen, Mag was close on his heels. He ran to the kitchen table. Hanging underneath this table were two double-barrelled breech-loading shotguns, loaded. They were a matching pair Pad had purchased from Jefferies of London, Gunmakers. Only one person outside the household knew they were hanging there. This was a character living down the road, that came to the house most nights, and had eaten Mag out of house and home. Also, on many nights had smoked Pad's last pipeful of tobacco.

O'Brien didn't hesitate, he put his hand under the table and took down the first gun. Mag got to grips with him at once, but in her present state she was no match for this treacherous cur. He wrenched the weapon from her hands and discharged both barrels over her head, through the kitchen window. She grabbed him again, this time by the hair of his head. He struck her a blow with the gun barrels across her swollen belly, and she fell, screaming with pain.

She would scream all that day and throughout the night. At eleven o'clock next morning her first son was prematurely delivered. By the grace of God, they both survived.

On the roadway Pad was no longer taking an interest in his surroundings. His attackers had removed the chains from a donkey's cart, and used these to bind him. With a piece of rope lashed underneath his armpits they began to tow him along the road leading to the village.

They had however forgotten to take one small detail into account. The wind being in the north, the shots were heard in the village. As the vigilantes were drawing near the town, the air was filled with the sound of gunfire, but the police had not had time to prepare a proper ambush, and the nine 'Freedom Fighters' made their escape through the fields and along hedges and ditches.

They left behind all their weapons.

When the first shots sounded, Pad came to his senses. While the commotion was in progress, he decided to make an attempt to escape. He was bound with chains from his shoulders to his knees, and therefore could not walk. He began to roll along the ground towards a stone wall. He got onto his knees and tumbled over this wall into a field, then rolled away from the area of the shooting. To the east of him was the river, and after a lot of effort and pain he reached its banks, and the doorway of a little house. The woman of this house, Madge McMahon, removed his chains and cleaned the wound. Later, she conveyed him home, and with another old neighbour spent the night nursing himself and his wife, until next morning the first son arrived before his time.

The 'Freedom Fighters' succeeded in bringing five of the Tongavauns to a farmhouse near Abbeyfeale. This was the venue for the trial. The man detailed to carry out this charade was imported from Cork. He came prepared to deal severely with criminals. When the full text of the case was revealed to him, he was thunderstruck.

Was it possible, that what was obviously a practical joke had led to this? He came, he said, from a county where the people were literally fighting with their backs to the wall against the greatest empire the world had ever known. Had they so much manpower and wealth at their disposal in this area, that they could afford to waste it in this fashion? Would they not be better employed if they turned their arms and manpower against the invader, and perhaps, in that way take some of the pressure off his native county? And with that parting remark, he stood up and left the farmhouse.

Two weeks after the round-up of the Tongavauns, the man that led the raiding party visited the fair in Newcastle West. On his way home, he was forced to take shelter from a thunderstorm in a blacksmith's forge. Several other people had also taken cover there from the torrential rain, amongst them a bosom pal of Jack Foley. At the sight of the raider, this man's hackles rose, and he grabbed him by the throat. In the ensuing struggle around the blacksmith's forge, with several men trying to loosen this powerful man's grip on the raider's neck, the saga of Jim the Lough's pigs reached its climax. When the two men were finally pulled apart, the leader of the round-up gang fell to the floor dead – his attacker had pulled the windpipe from his throat.

When the lump in Jack Foley's neck burst and killed him, there followed in the village a strange series of incidents.

His only relation was a widowed sister, living in a neighbouring parish. She had two sons, both former members of the Royal Irish Constabulary.

When Jack had been laid to rest and his affairs wound up, his sister was in the process of cleaning out the pub, where spring-cleaning, or indeed any other seasonal clean-out, had been rare as live rabbits in a ferret box. She was anticipating a visit from two brothers who had made a tentative offer of six hundred pounds for the pub. These brothers had been paid off by their father from a farm in West Limerick. The father, wishing to parcel out his estate, gave the family holding to the first-born son, and settled a sum of money on the other two.

The widow was to receive a disappointment however. Instead of two visitors, she had in fact three, and none of them bore any resemblance to the brothers. Her three visitors were loyal supporters of Sinn Fein. One was the most substantial businessman in the village. Number Two was a first-rate tradesman, and the third was what might be called a displaced person. He came from a large family of boys. His parents owned a farm, but there was no room for this one.

The three men didn't beat about the bush. They told the widow quite bluntly that she was to receive sixty pounds for the pub, and she didn't have any choice in the matter. The widow told them just as frankly to 'kiss her arse', and get out fast before someone got hurt. The cold, calm, and deadly reply chilled her to the bone.

She would do well to consider her situation, they told her. It was a well-known fact that two of her sons were Black and Tans. The fact that they were now left the country didn't mean it was not possible to have them 'dealt with'. She was getting sixty pounds, and she had better take it. If not, she'd get nothing at all. If she tried to go against them they would see that she was boycotted.

One might wonder why the woman didn't go for the Law and have these three gangsters arrested, but the Free State was not long in existence, and memories were not so short as to forget the excesses of the security forces during the liberation struggle. The woman took the money, and in a short while the displaced farmer took up residence in the pub.

When the widow left her brother's public house for the last time, she visited the local Chapel. In the yard adjoining the House of God was a huge cross, bearing the image of the crucified Christ. The woman knelt beneath this cross for a long time. Soon she was weeping, and she cried her tale of woe to the righter of all wrongs. 'I cannot deal with them,' she sobbed. 'I'm an old woman, widowed and heart scalded. I leave them in your capable hands . . . '

The new owner of Foley's pub went from strength to strength. Not only did most drinkers of the village support him, but also visitors from the outlying areas. After all was he not a famous Freedom Fighter? Had he not spent time in prison for Ireland's cause?

Alas, all this hero worship proved too much for our new Publican, and he began to commit the unpardonable sin of any landlord: he began to take drink inside his own counter. When drunk, he became a garrulous and insulting ruffian. Customers were told they were not fit to stand in the same room with such as he. During the war of attrition against the invaders, had he not led numerous attacks against Tans and Police? People soon tired of these repetitive tales, and began to drift away, first in ones and twos, then in groups until finally the porter went sour and rotted in the barrels, and wisps of grass and weeds began to appear round the jambs of the door.

The substantial businessman was prospering. He raised money from the bank and expanded his premises. He carried a large stock of wares, and could at twenty-four hours' notice supply any article required for home or farm.

During his sleep, one night, he had a strange dream: people were shouting at him, and the word they were repeating again and again was 'fire'. Suddenly he awoke, only to find that what he thought was a dream was in fact a real nightmare. His premises were on fire from end to end, and he was forced to jump for his life from an upstairs window, in his night clothes. The remainder of his household were jumping through other windows, and they now gathered on the street, in the company of neighbours to watch the inferno. By morning, all that remained was rubble and smouldering ruins.

Worse was to follow. This 'intelligent' man had not carried a penny's insurance on his property. In a short while he was to be seen scouring the countryside in search of a day's work, and soon was reduced to beggary.

The tradesman? He too had a date with the righter of all wrongs. His brother had purchased a colt, and had him shod by the local smith. While the tradesman was visiting one evening, his brother asked him to examine the horse, as he felt the shoes were over-tight, and the animal was showing signs of lameness. The tradesman went to the yard where the horse was confined, and stooping, examined his fetlocks. The animal lashed once, with his newly-shod hind leg. and struck the tradesman between the eyes.

When a doctor finally got to the scene, he found him lying quite dead, his skull in pulp . . .

Four

It's Saturday, thank God, and we're loading the puntgun bright and early. It is our intention to visit the sandbar off Aughenish Island. We have seen widgeon packing there, and were waiting for a break in the weather to pay them a visit. You don't travel far in a shooting punt in foul weather. Frost, with its accompanying calm weather conditions, is what's needed. With only a few inches of clear board on a shooting punt, you dare not take chances.

As this will be a full day's outing, we've loaded both barrels. The left is loaded with BB shot; this is for geese or duck. The second barrel has snipe-shot; we are hoping for a blow at golden plover. These birds are Pad's favourites. If you should meet them in large numbers, standing close together, this weapon will cut roads through them. Their attraction for Pad is financial: they fetch four shillings and sixpence each. If you get a good shot, it helps pay the rent for some time.

Puntgunners, writing on their subject, have mentioned good shots at duck and geese while these birds were sitting on the water. I must say I find these statements hard to swallow. In our experience, when you attempt to punt into these fowl, they will on most occasions swim away as fast as they can, and while doing so spread out and make it impossible to get a good shot. We have long since given up this system, and confine our shooting to fowl standing feeding on the mudbanks.

When I first began to travel in the punt with Pad I made my share of mistakes, like all beginners. We put one and a half pounds of snipe-shot nicely through a flock of green and golden plover that were feeding on Hayes's Marsh on a Christmas day, and left the area littered with dead and wounded birds. I was detailed to jump out and catch as many 'wounders' as possible before they had time to hide in the ricegrass and trenches. Pad would pick any birds floating on the water. These had fallen from the flock after the shot. The dead birds lying on the marsh were left 'til last: these were safe, and certainly weren't going anywhere.

I duly began chasing after wounded plover, and when both hands were full, I ran onto dry land and dropped them there, and immediately returned to the chase on the marsh and a repeat performance.

Pad was shouting something from the punt, but I hadn't time to listen, there were plover running everywhere. The place where I was throwing the wounders was called Shanna Walla, and at the time was covered with furze and ferns. I had made several trips to the shore before I realised what Pad was shouting across the marsh: 'You bloody clown, they're all running away.'

In the excitement of the chase I had forgotten to twist the necks of the plover I was taking ashore, and they were now safely hidden in the ferns and furze of Shanna Walla. I have never lived it down.

Nevertheless, we brought home from that one shot, one hundred and twenty-nine birds.

Saturday is my favourite day of the week, and one can look forward to two full days of shooting, and no worries about Old Rooney and his ashplant.

We're now heading across Bohaun mudbanks and facing west. How this area ever got such a name I have not been able to ascertain. The name means literally 'cowdung'. Perhaps the fishermen that were obliged to walk through it in the course of their profession felt it resembled that unsavoury product.

Around us, all the landmarks carry the ancient Irish names. In spite of attempts by the invader to translate them, some defied translation. The beautiful Irish names ripple off the tongue like music. Due north lies the massive rock of Carrig Eire Vaun; off its northern point is Eanna Eire Vaun. To the east is the little island of Coneela; south is the huge rock, Carrig Preachain, where the scal crow has come to feed on the mussels since time began. The banks of empty shells piled high around its base are ample proof of their success. How did they first come to learn that to pick a mussel from the rocks and fly with it to a certain height, and then drop it onto the great rock, they would get themselves a meal?

West of Carrig Preachain is Tieret; north of that is Cly Bawn mudbank; west again, Trumra Mor, and Trumra Beag. South of here is Poul Na Roan; west of that, Cos Thine; south, Uisce Bheal; the list is endless. Out here on the wide expanse of the Shannon Estuary, one can begin to understand the loss to a nation of its native language.

Two miles to the south, in Cullawilen Bay, the sky has suddenly darkened with thousands of green and golden plover. The hunting hawks have come out of the ruined castle of Toomdeely in search of prey. These killers of the sky have used the ruins for centuries. Perhaps in the company of the spirits of the bishops that legend tells us were their former denizens.

These hawks seem to have a preference for green plover, above all else. This proud little bird can be very deceptive in its movements. One might observe it during the daytime, flapping lazily over fields and gardens, and perhaps, for this reason has been given the name 'lapwing'. But towards nightfall, its movements take on a new dimension and it can be seen hurtling across the sky like a shooting star. In size and weight it is slightly bigger than the hawk, yet this hunter can pick a plover from the air with its talons and fly back to its castle ruins with the still-flapping bird held securely.

The hawks have often been instrumental in providing us with a puntgun shot. When the plover are perched on a marsh, perhaps several miles from the water, and there is no possible way of getting close enough for a shot, along comes the hawk and drives them wildly into the Estuary. Then, after searching round for a likely landing-place, they begin to pour from the sky onto the sloblands, and stand thick as the grass along the water's edge. The golden plover at this time, when he finds the tide rising round his legs, will commence his beautiful music. While waiting in the punt under cover of a seaweed rock, allowing the birds time to settle before our approach, I have watched Pad's face, as he appeared to become enchanted with that heavenly sound, and under his breath he would murmur, 'God's blessings on your sweet note.'

The black-backed gull can also be a help, but other times he can be the cause of losing you a good shot. He will attack the packs of duck and chase them along the river, searching out the weak or wounded birds in the flock. He very soon separates these from the main bunch, and then pounces on his chosen victim. When he begins his attack, he can be the means of driving the duck within range of your gun; then again, he might just take the notion to swoop on a pack of duck you have been punting into for several miles, and might just now be almost within range. Suddenly this scavanger swoops, and scatters the duck far and wide.

At these times, I have heard this bird called names that really suggested his ancestry was a mess.

We have reached the channel running west of Trumra, and we're now heading for the Carrigeens and Greenaans. This area can usually be relied on for a pack of duck. We begin to prepare the punt. It is too late for this when the birds are in sight; as I've said before, they probably will also have seen you, and taken to their heels. It might seem strange that wildfowl feeding on a mudbank take so little notice of a shooting punt, provided there is no sign of life on board. Their main fear seems to be the land, and of course this is to the advantage of the wildfowler. A shooting punt, moving slowly on the water, painted slate-grey to tone in with its surrounds, holds no fear for them.

We round the reef of Trumra, and north-west of us, a quarter mile away, a pack of widgeon are feeding on the gravel.

If there is one thing that has cost puntgunners dear, it is greed. When approaching a pack of duck, if you come upon a smaller flock, perhaps fifty or sixty yards closer to you, what action are you supposed to take? If you attempt to pass out the smaller lot to reach the main flock, more than likely these will rise and carry the lot with them.

We are now faced with this situation. In the main bunch feeding near the Greenaans are surely several thousand widgeon. Betwen us and them is a smaller flock of mixed duck, perhaps two hundred strong. For Pad there is no choice: we'll go for the smaller lot, a duck in the punt is worth several on the mussel bank.

I am again struggling to get as far away from the gun as I can. We are moving fast with the tide, and I have the string held tight in my right hand, ready to fire at the signal of command.

It is difficult to describe the feeling in your breast as you lie face down on the bottom of a shooting punt, with the butt of that murderous gun over your head, and all around you the voices of thousands of wild things, talking that strange language that only their own kind understand. Never guessing for one moment that a mighty thunderclap is about to devastate them.

A sharp kick brings me back from my reverie, and at the same instant I pull the string. The explosion again sets my head ringing, and I stand up and stagger back towards Pad. But there is no time to waste. Get the double-barrel shoulder-gun, and start shooting 'wounders'.

A duck wounded in the water doesn't give you much time for making buttons, he is trying to get away as fast as he can. In a few minutes, I have shot nine widgeon that were swimming and diving trying to escape. We don't bother with the dead ones for the moment. When no more duck are to be seen on the water, Pad brings the punt to the gravel, and I get out and pick up the dead birds. These are packed under the deck of the punt. I have counted thirty-six widgeon and eight shovellers. Not bad, from a small flock. Talking of what might have happened from a shot at the main flock is a futile business.

Immediately the sound of the shot dies away, the air over the punt is filled with gulls. These scavengers have come to realise that the noise of the gun can mean food. Even now, away in the distance, several groups of seagulls are fighting over the remains of two duck that fell from the flock after the shot.

Pad fills his pipe. He looks contented, sitting on the stern of the punt. I get a few rags and clean the blood and mud from the floorboards, we don't want to lie on that. We are waiting for low water and the flood tide, to begin our return journey to the area where the plover darkened the sky this morning. Strange, that even the attention of the hawks didn't force them to abandon Hewson's Marsh. Pad looks towards the north-east, and wrinkles his nose. 'You'll get frost,' he said. 'I can feel the sting of it on the tips of my toes. That's why the plover are not coming out. We'll go up with the tide and hope for a crack at them before dark.'

We sit and wait for the tide, and my mind begins to wander. Two years before, at this spot, we were punting into a flock of brent geese. I was in my usual position, lying down, facing the floorboards. Pad was lying on his back punting, when suddenly a snort at my ear makes me turn, and I almost bump my nose into the face of a seal. It was difficult to know who got the worst fright, me or the seal. At any rate, I let out a roar that sent the unfortunate animal away, diving and plunging through the water, in the general direction of the Beeves Lighthouse, emitting strange barks and bleats. At the same time our flock of brent geese was heading for the Clare shore as fast as their wings would take them.

Pad sat up on the stern of the punt, put his chin on his chest, and shook his head from side to side, in his own fashion. I couldn't be sure if he was laughing or crying. It was only now becoming obvious that the seal, seeing the strange object on the water, was overcome with curiosity, and stuck his head over the coaming of the punt to have a peep. We have not seen him around this locality since.

At last the tide turns, and we begin to move with it. It is essential, when shooting wildfowl, be it duck, geese, plover, or whatever, that the punt is on a correspondent level with the flock. Using the rest, you can raise the muzzle, but if the birds are standing on a high marsh, you may find the charge passes harmlessly over their heads. This is the situation

"I let out a roar that sent the unfortunate animal
diving and plunging through the water...."

now on Hewson's Marsh. We are within range of the golden plover. They are standing packed together, singing their plover song, but we can't fire on them. The tide is too low, and we must wait for more water.

Lying in a punt, barefooted, in freezing weather, is a painful job. You dare not make a move, and as the pins and needles take hold, you begin to feel very sorry for yourself. The tide seems to rise slowly: a watched pot never boils. It is now beginning to get dark, and the plover could decide to leave for the overnight quarters at any moment.

Pad is sighting along the barrels of the great gun. He whispers to me under his breath, 'Get ready, they're getting restless.' He waits a few more seconds, then, 'Let them have it.' The murderous weapon roars, and a pound and a half of snipe-shot leaves the barrel and sweeps through the plover like a scythe through corn. The shot would have been better if the tide was higher, but 'if ifs and ands were pots and pans, what would the tinkers do?' We picked up ninety-six golden plover, three curlew and four redshank.

My feet have regained some feeling, and I'm looking forward to getting home. We are having a pot of green plover, boiled with turnips; the thought makes my teeth water in anticipation, and I pull harder and harder with the paddles. Pad is working hard on the stern with the punting paddle, I suppose he gets hungry too, sometimes.

Sunday morning is a busy time around here. It is then the fowlers from the City arrive to chance their luck and skill at the 'Fowler Rock' flight. These rocks span the entrance to Culawillen Bay, and are uncovered at half-tide. When four or five guns are placed at strategic points along these rocks, the results can be devastating. You don't need any beginners here. The flocks of duck come tearing out of the bay as if the Devil from Hell was hot on their heels. Many a so-called sharpshooter has come here, only to return home in the afternoon with cartridge bag empty, and gamebag light. As Pad has often put it, 'firing at the wind'.

Three Sundays previously, a city gent arrived, bringing with him a nephew, just released from a famous sporting college in England, to spend his holidays in the land of his forefathers. During his long wearisome nights in that house of learning, the nephew had borrowed from the house library, the masterpiece, Ralph Payne Gallwey's *The Fowler in Ireland*. From that moment, he longed for the opportunity to put into practice what he had so avidly read from the pen of that great man. He prevailed on Pad – much against the latter's better judgement – to take him in the punt, in the hope of getting a shot. I travelled in the Gandalo with the uncle, taking care to remain well in the background.

38

Under the steep mudbank of Lan Tighe, a small pack of widgeon were sheltering. The puntgunners prepared to attack. It was explained to the young man that when the fateful moment arrived, he would receive the time-honoured signal, a kick in the pants. Unfortunately, while attempting to keep the bow of the punt turned into the wind, Pad accidentally gave the lad a dart with his heel. The young man immediately pulled the string.

When the gun went off they were well out of range. Also, the gun was pointing in the wrong direction. When we reached them, Pad was sitting on the stern, his chin on his chest, shaking his head from side to side. 'Jesus look down on me,' he said. 'Jesus look down on me.'

My weekend has fled on wings of ecstasy. It is Monday again, and I must hit the road for the schoolhouse.

Five

For a change, this Monday morning sees me arrive on time, and I can sit at the desk with Jim Brody and listen to some other boys putting forward their preposterous excuses for their late arrival.

Today, for a start, we will have an hour of religious instruction. Old Rooney points the ashplant at a boy in the back row. 'Give me the first line of the Lord's Prayer,' he said.

The lad begins in a shaky voice. 'Our Father which art in Heaven . . . '

'All right,' Rooney tells him. 'Next boy carry on from there.'

'Hallowed be Thy name.' 'Next boy.'

'Thy kingdom come.' 'Next.'

'Thy will be done.' 'Very good. Next.'

'On earth as it is in Heaven.'

Old Rooney points at a lad, sitting some distance in front of me, 'What about you, yes, you with the Eskimo hair cut.'

The boy stands up and wrings his hands, then blurts out, 'The bite to ate, sir.'

Old Rooney stretches his arms before him on the rostrum, and lowers his head onto his left elbow. He remained like that for several moments. I couldn't swear it, but I got the feeling he was laughing.

This boy he referred to as the Eskimo could always be relied on for this type of answer, but the Master never laid a finger on him. The boy's responses were outlandish, but usually had some bearing on the subject in hand.

He lived in the village with his grandparents. He was an only child. His parents, who had lived in a little cabin in a lane off the main street, decided one night they had had enough, and left him at the door of his grandparents' house; it was the last ever seen of them. He had very soon picked up all the quaint sayings and mannerisms of the old couple. His

40

name was Thomas Cannon, and except for his old-fashioned sayings, he was bright as a button.

His grandmother had had her left eye knocked out with a blow of an ashplant during a horse fair in Rathkeale several years previously. She had gone to the assistance of her husband Jimmy, who was embroiled in a fight with some tinkers over the sale of a horse.

As fate would have it, Jimmy had also lost an eye while cutting scallops in Ballyclough Wood some time before. It was a bad stroke of luck, as he had just returned home having fought through the First World War without the Germans being able to put a scratch on him. The British, too, failed to give him a shilling in compensation for those four terrible years. His wife Mary was inclined to call him the one-eyed gunner, and he would reply that she was a 'hairy ould pot to call the kettle black arse'.

Mary smoked a clay pipe with just a little stem, which she called a 'dudeen'; more times she referred to it as a 'jaw-warmer'. She had an unquenchable thirst for porter, and was quite prepared to sell her soul for this black lady with the blonde head.

She had touched most residents of the area with her schemes and cunning to obtain money. As time passed her field of operations narrowed, until one Saturday night she came to the end of her rope. She took herself to the Chapel and entered the confession box where the Parish Priest was sitting, with his head pounding from the constant stream of 'meaws' pouring their tales of misery into his ears.

When he pulled the slide on the grille and recognised the outline of his visitor, a little warning-bell sounded in his already overloaded brain. It could not be said by any means that Mary had a track worn to the Chapel, her presence could only mean trouble. It was not only by reputation she was known to the PP, she had burned him many times in the past. As she was mumbling away through the grille, his mind was racing ahead. What would she try this time? The silence brought him back with a jerk, and he realised she was finished. Perhaps he was wronging her.

He raised his hand and gave her his blessing, but before he was finished she broke into his prayer.

'Hold on a minute, Father,' she said. 'My soul is very troubled.'

'What is it?' he said testily.

'I stole five shillings,' she said, 'and I'd be afraid to go to the rails in the morning because of it.'

The old priest peered through the grille at her face trying to read her

41

thoughts. 'Don't worry about it, mam,' he said. 'I'm sure when you have the money you'll pay it back.'

'Well, I'll tell you, Father,' she said, 'I was hoping you'd give me the loan of it, and I'd pay it back tonight.'

At the opposite side of the box Jim Brody's uncle was waiting his turn. With an effort he choked down the burst of laughter that rose in his throat. 'Twas a good try, Mary, he thought, a good try.

She was facing back towards the village. If she was a crying woman she'd have been shedding tears of frustration, but she knew this was no good, you needed money to buy porter. Well, the Son of a Whore, what did he mean he was a bit short at the moment? Didn't every fool know they were rolling in it? Whenever they wanted money, all they had to do was threaten the people with the Devil, and they soon coughed up. Christ Almighty, the nature was gone out of the Irish.

She got back to the village with her porter-thirst raging worse than ever, and her fertile brain working at full-steam. She entered Brogs' butcher's stall and went through to the yard where a barrel was filled with bones left over from his trade. She picked out a few rib-bones of a sheep and brought these round the corner to her little house in the lane. A few chops with a hatchet and the bones were the desired length.

Mary soon had a tidy little parcel under her arm and was heading back for the street. She entered a draper's shop near the corner. The owner of this shop was a spinster whose sister was married to a farmer outside the village.

'God save you, miss.' 'And you too, Mary. And what can I do for you?' 'Your brother-in-law called to the house this morning and told me I was to leave in a dozen of fresh herrings here for him. He said you'd pay me, miss.'

'That's fine,' the spinster told her. 'What's the charge, Mary?' 'A half-crown, miss.'

Mary and Jimmy had applied for the blind pension. One might think the act of having only one eye would immediately qualify them for this, not so. There was, and still is, in this area what is known as a pension committee. This committee is comprised of people from the better-off section of the community, and unlikely to find themselves reduced to the form of beggary which is part and parcel of being brought before this group.

The old couple were only too well aware of what they were up against. On the appointed day, they were told to take themselves to the upstairs room of the Carnegie Library which stood on the Quay overlooking the River Deel. The old couple prepared carefully for their trial. Each would take a stout stick to help them find their way. Jimmy had told his wife that when they got to the Library door, she was to trip him. Mary duly tripped him, and he tumbled in a heap into the room where the pension committee waited to pass judgement on their case. He was picked off the floor and dusted down, before the long and arduous cross-examination began.

'I believe ye own a donkey and cart?' 'That's right, sir.' 'What do ye use this for?' 'Selling fish around the country, whenever we can get them.'

The fellow asking most of the questions got up from the table and walked to the window. He gazed across the river towards Pelkinton's Hill, then he called Jimmy to join him. 'Tell me,' he said, 'is that a bush over there?' The old man gazed across the river to where the committeeman was pointing. 'Blasht me,' he said, 'are you trying to take the sight out of my good eye? Isn't that Croneen's ould pony?'

They returned empty-handed to the little house in the lane, the committee had not been impressed by their case. Mary had one old pair of shoes she wears out of doors; at home she went barefoot. She was now busy round the fire preparing their evening meal. It was simple fare: a saucepan of onions thickened with flour boiling away near the fire; hanging on the pothooks was the little black pot of potatoes. She went to poke the fire, and Jimmy moved his feet out of her way. Unfortunately he wasn't very careful where he put his steel-shod boots, and almost removed one of her big toes. She lit the kitchen with oaths and curses. 'You blind bastard!' she shouted. 'You could see Croneen's ould pony and you can't see my misfortunate toes!'

This last cut got Jimmy riled. 'Woman,' he said, 'you've no respect for your husband. If you keep going as you are, I'll do you in, do you hear me? I'll do you in, and there won't be anything done to me because I'll 'list straight away. You better realise, my good woman, that I'm King of this castle and I want no more of your bad talk.'

Mary looked at him for a moment. 'Are you really the King?' she said. 'Because in that case I'd better crown you,' and she reached for the saucepan of boiling onions and turned it upside-down on his head.

Sitting on the same seat as Thomas Cannon is a boy with the nickname, 'Little Big Toe'. This name was appropriate, as the boy in question had the most peculiar toes. When you were sitting well down the classroom you had a good view of all the bare legs of the boys sticking back underneath the desks. Most feet were riddled with new and old scars, my own being no exception. My toes had become so

43

splayed from constantly going without shoes or boots that I had gained the name 'Paddle Toes'. But Little Big Toe was a different case. His feet had not become this shape from going without boots, he was born without the normal big toes. His little toes were situated where the big ones should have been, and this gave a most peculiar appearance to his feet. It didn't seem to bother him much: he had a very slight limp, but otherwise was quite normal.

His father had died the previous year. He had the distinction, or misfortune, depending on your point of view, of leaving this vale of tears on the same night as the Parish Priest.

This PP was a man of immense proportions, and to add to his troubles, had suffered for many years with that abominable scourge called the gout.

He was also plagued by a blacksmith living at the eastern end of the village. This blacksmith had a niece teaching in the National School at Newcastle and for many years he'd tried to obtain a position for her in the local school of her home parish. As the PP was the school manager, the smith looked to him to use his influence to have the niece placed in the first vacancy that would occur. However, the priest had relations of his own in the teaching profession, and placed one of these in the first vacant position.

The smith's anger knew no bounds at what he considered this affront. He took himself to a watering-place and charged his batteries, then with a stout blackthorn stick in his fist he made a beeline for the PP's house. When he reached that lofty residence, it could not be said he was in an amiable mood. He attacked the hall door like a battering-ram and almost took it off its hinges.

When the startled housekeeper came to investigate, the smith got straight to the point. 'Send out that big bastard, I want him,' he shouted, waving the blackthorn in her face. What the smith didn't realise was, the PP had him under observation from a side window, and when he now approached his front door, he brought with him his own stout blackthorn.

'What do you mean,' shouted the smith, 'bringing your relations from all over the country to fill the jobs in this village, and the native has to clear out, you bandy-legged bastard.'

The PP had suffered enough from the gout eating away at his feet without being ridiculed about his lameness, and he made a swipe with his stick at the smith's head. The blacksmith did not in the least resemble the usual image one might have of a man following this strenuous profession. He was small and wiry, and like a cat on his feet. He sprang back from the intended blow and parried the priest's stick with his own.

There now followed on the village street a scene reminiscent of the lion and mouse fable. The huge figure of the priest, hobbling on his gout-torn feet, and bellowing like a bull, forcing the little wiry blacksmith to retreat down the village. The crash of blackthorns as the two men tried to outmanoeuvre each other brought the inhabitants from their houses. The smith was getting more than he bargained for, and, probably from the strenuous exercise, he now found that the false strength of the porter was beginning to desert him. From the corner of his eye he saw a baldy-headed publican, standing out on the street wiping his hands, and watching the strange stick fight with several others. The smith had often spent his last shilling in those premises, and he now believed he might get succour there. Suddenly he dropped the stick and bolted for the pub door. The publican however did not wish to become embroiled in this feud, and he ran into the shop and banged the door in the face of the smith. The little man hammered with his fists on the door and shouted, 'Jasus, let me in quick, there's a ton weight of a saint after me.'

He needn't have hurried, the PP had had enough too, and was sitting on a shop window across the street, suffering damnation from the recent strain he had inflicted on his legs.

Little Big Toe's father and this Parish Priest lay side by side, in two brown boxes, in the centre aisle of the chapel. On the day of the funeral, a High Mass would be sung for the deceased priest. Before the sacrament commenced, the acting PP approached the Clerk of the Chapel, and he in turn rounded up a few of the congregation. Two chairs were placed in the yard at the side of the Chapel, and the coffin containing the mortal remains of Little Big Toe's father was brought out and placed on these. The incident provoked a character in the village to mix a bucket of whitewash, and two nights later he wrote on the Chapel wall: *High Mass For High Money, Low Mass For Low Money, And NO Mass for NO Money.*

Six

Down the road from us is a bachelor farm. It holds within its doubtful boundary inbred remnants of an Elfish dynasty. Their ability to farm was nil. They employed a farm worker from the west coast of Clare. He was red of face and hair as well as being a notorious 'Geocock'. He was given free rein to run the farm as he saw fit. As farm-workers go, he was second to none. When he arrived at the farm, the two little bachelor brothers and spinster sister were hard put to find enough to eat. The Clareman could turn his hand to any task. He shod horses, thatched the dwelling-house and outhouses, repaired farm machinery, ploughed, tilled and planted the fields. Also he took over the buying and selling of animals. In a few years he turned what had almost become a derelict homestead into a model farm. He did in fact spend the remainder of his working life there, which spanned almost thirty-seven years.

When the last of the family passed on to the great farm in the sky, without making any provision for that outstanding workman, a long-forgotten niece, living in America, returned to the land of her fathers. She was bred and born in that vast land, and when word reached her of the Irish situation, she decided a trip might be to her advantage.

She arrived by taxi at nightfall. It was a wet and dismal January evening when the Irish countryside takes on that gloomy dour appearance which sends shivers running along the backs of visitors from the warm climes. When she left the warmth and safety of the car and ventured a few paces into the farmyard, she stood in awe, and gazed round at the thatched buildings. She began to mutter to herself. 'Surely this cannot be the place, surely my aunt and uncles didn't spend their lives here?'

The Clareman, being attracted hither by the sound of the car, emerged from a shed where he had been milking a cow by the light of a

46

candle. He approached the immaculately-dressed woman standing in the yard. It has to be admitted, he was a rough-looking character at the best of times. Now, dressed in his working clothes, the sight of him proved too much for the American visitor and she turned and bolted back to the taxi as fast as her legs would carry her, while at her heels a huge sheepdog was prancing and growling as if about to devour her.

She would not stand at the farm again. Next day she entered the offices of the family solicitors in the city where she established her bona fides as next of kin. A week later the farm was put up for sale. The Clareman was given twenty-four hours to vacate the house, and he returned to Clare in the same condition as he had arrived here thirty-seven years previously, his total possessions, the clothes on his back.

When he departed, few tears were shed. He had, during his term of residence, succeeded in drawing the wrath of every family in the district down on his head; as I've said, he was a thundering Geocock, foul-mouthed and belligerent.

He was a firm believer in the power of pishoguery. It might be hard to swallow now, but he was terrified of red-headed women. This attitude was widespread in parts of the country at the time. Where or how it first originated I'm not in a position to say. If this powerfully-built man happened to journey to the hinterland for any purpose, and came on the path of a red-headed woman, he would immediately retrace his steps, completely convinced that, should he continue, some terrible calamity would befall him. He seemed to have missed the fact that he was walking around with the same danger on top of his head in the shape of his own red locks.

He was also wary of whitethorn forts. Some years previously, a chap from the village had cut a huge whitethorn tree in one such fort, and during his efforts to drag it home for the fire, had obviously strained his heart and died shortly afterwards. The Clareman, who was sitting at our fireside when he got the news, struck the table a lash with his fist and shouted, 'Now who has the last laugh? What am I always telling ye about interfering with forts?'

In spite of his foul language and cantankerous nature, the mother had, as she put it, a 'graw' for him. Some years previously when my young sister was dying of diptheria, he arrived at our house in the small hours of the morning, and tapping at the back window, he produced a bag of bull's-eyes he had been carrying about with him throughout the day (they were now melted into a solid lump). In a drunken slur he mumbled through the window, 'They're for the young lady.' From that day on he could do no wrong in our house.

He had delivered and received some terrible beatings during his term in the West Limerick village. His right hand was partly mutilated. During a fracas on the village bridge he had made swipe at a village lout that happened to remark on the close resemblance between the greyhound the Clareman was walking at the time and a mongrel sheepdog that had just passed. Fortunately for the lout, and unfortunately for the Clareman, the former could duck faster than the latter could punch, and the intended blow landed on the stone parapet of the bridge shattering the two middle fingers of his right hand. Within twenty-four hours they had to be removed by operation at Croom Hospital.

The greyhound the Clareman was walking at the time of the fracas was known as Delia the Dasher. The previous Friday night, he had taken her, in the company of several other dogs, and characters, from the village, to Limerick Dog Track for a trial. The hound was in fact a flyer, and in later years was to win many races. But now, being merely a beginner, like all beginners was apt to make mistakes.

When the race was in progress, the Clareman got himself into position near the fnish line, to cheer on his hound. As the hare rounded into the finishing stretch of the track, and it was plainly seen that Delia was in front and streaking away from the rest of the pack, the excitement got too much for the Clareman. He whipped off his cap, and whirling it round his head, shouted at the top of his voice, 'Come on, Delia.' The call echoed over the heads of the assembled throng and reached the speeding Delia. How could she mistake that raucous voice.

She immediately applied all brakes and came to a sudden stop, looking round for the source of that call. The remaining hounds streaked past her over the finish line.

An English visitor, a famous lady greyhound-breeder, was standing near the Clareman. She looked at him in amazement. 'Whatever must have happened to that dog?' she said.

He rounded on her savagely. 'Ah!' he said. 'She stopped to make her shit.'

The farm adjoining the Clareman's place of employment was owned by Jim Brody's family. He made their lives a hell on earth. He reserved a special quota of venom for a little workman employed there for many years. He was originally a spailpeen, a travelling farm-worker, and had come hither many years previously with the tools of his trade strapped to his back, a garden spade and reaping-hook.

In appearance, he was the very opposite to the Clareman. He was tiny in stature and neat as tuppence, and very soon was given the nickname

'Spanker'. He had the strange habit when speaking of rarely completing a sentence without using the expression 'I turned around'. Spanker could 'oblige' crops to grow in a garden, where other men of the land couldn't grow weeds. This played no small part in aggravating the relationship between himself and the Clareman.

On my way to the shore one evening, with my muzzle-loader under my arm, and Fly hopping along behind, I noticed in the distance a man stooping behind a ditch, peeping through the bushes into the garden beyond. As I drew near I recognised the Clareman. He also had seen me, and was now waving his cap at me to keep down. I duly made myself small, and very soon reached the ditch where he was peeping into the next field. I soon saw the source of his curiosity. The Spanker was in the garden planting potatoes. He was setting them 'under the bub'. This means placing seed potatoes in the drill, and covering them with a small amount of earth from the side of the furrow. After a few weeks, when they are about to shoot, the manure is put in and the drill is closed. It is believed that this hurries the process of germination.

As it was near nightfall, and I'd hoped to get the evening flight of duck, I told the Clareman I'd have to leave. 'Wait a minute,' he said. 'Jasus, wait a minute.' As he was talking, Spanker gathered up his tools and left for home. As soon as he was over the end wall of the garden and drawing away into the twilight, the Clareman pulled a sack from under his coat, vaulted the ditch, and began picking every second spud from under the bub.

Several months later, when I overheard the little spailpeen telling Pad that he turned around and planted a garden of early potatoes, and now, when he turned around and went to have a look at them, only every second one was growing, but he was going to turn around and pay a visit to the chap that supplied the dud seed, and he would turn around and give him a piece of his mind. I walked hurriedly away. I have to admit that at the time I thought it was very funny. Now I'm not so sure.

These two workmen were the exceptions to the majority of farm-hands in the region. Some of the farmers treated their workmen, or as they were called, 'farmers' boys' – their age didn't matter, they were all 'farmers' boys' – in the same category as the sheepdogs.

It must surely be a source of wonder to people with a knowledge of the time, that a variety of the Biblical plagues were not visited on the farming community in retaliation for the blackguarding and ill treatment they meted out to 'servant boys' and 'servant girls'.

They hired out in this region, usually for eleven months, at the

January fair in Newcastle West. From early morning, they would gather in the square of this West Limerick town, from all over the county, and as far afield as Cork and North Kerry. There, they would shelter along the walls of the buildings, and the farmers examined them as if they were beasts of the field, feeling the girls' bodies through their clothing, to ascertain if they had the physique suitable for slaving on the land. These girls would not hire out merely for housework, but indeed, for all types of farm work.

They rarely slept in the farmhouse proper. Usually, some shed in the yard was touched up for this purpose, probably the barn, and there, on a makeshift bed, or beds, they would sleep. Lest one might think that this was a glorious opportunity for sexual encounters, the amount of work these people were obliged to perform left very little energy for any other type of performance. They would not be allowed to sit at table during mealtimes with other members of the family. They took their meals in the back kitchen. If they were lucky, they had a table for this purpose; usually the meal was eaten off a box.

Some time before the incident of the spailpeen, I had been dispatched in the boat across the river to collect a broody hen from the farmer living near Tom Saucepan's house. The farmer's wife informed me that the hen was confined in the barn, and as she was busy, I could go myself and collect it. I duly went to the barn where I found the hen busily putting the finishing touches to a nest of straw on top of a horse's cart. The cart was wedged into a corner behind the barn door, and even at first glance, there appeared something unusual about it. On further examination, I found it was in fact being used as a bed. It consisted of three sacks of straw and several cast-off top coats.

On arriving home and relating my story to Pad, he could hardly believe it. However, on making further enquiries, he learned that this was indeed the living-quarters of the workman, and he had survived there through some of the worst winters on record.

This particular farmer had an elder sister a nun; the younger brother was a priest. At the time in Ireland, it was the ambition of every mother to have a son a priest. If a daughter should enter a convent and become a nun, so much the better; the family's standing in the community was that much more enhanced. The fact that in fifty per cent of the cases it was the mother had the vocation didn't matter an iota. Many a boy and girl were railroaded into seminaries and convents in their childhood, only to awaken in later years to a situation and lifestyle for which they were never suited.

50

Shortly after collecting the broody hen, I was repairing a boat, down on the quay with Pad, when this same priest and nun came walking along the riverbank. They had been home for some time attending a family wedding, and were now taking the air on what was then a favourite walk. They remained for some time, chatting on various topics.

Suddenly the young priest turned to my father and remarked, 'I believe, Pad, you're not a great one for Mass and the Sacraments?'

My father laid down his hammer and turned to face the priest. 'You believe right,' he said. 'I suppose you people have your scouts out, checking up on old sinners like me? It's a pity you don't send some of them into the barn where your brother keeps his workman.'

The nun flushed scarlet, then her face drained, and she turned quite pale. The only reaction from the priest for a moment, was to scrape the toe of his shoe backwards and forwards on the grass, then he looked at my father and smiled.

'Pad,' he said, 'did you ever read the New Testament?'

Pad looked at him in surprise, and said, 'I read bits of it, here and there.'

'Well,' continued the priest, 'did you read the bit where it said Our Lord was born in a stable, between an ox and an ass? And you know, Pad, Our Lord was the Divine Son of God.'

My father was a man slow to anger. He had long since learned its futility. But now I saw his jowls begin to tremble, and his face became white as chalk.

'Do you know something?' he said. 'Ever since I came out of the shell I've been listening to that convenient answer from priests and wealthy lay-people. The Irish have a very flexible conscience when it comes to the poor. Would you not think,' he went on, 'the message God was trying to convey to us by that strange happening was conveniently misconstrued? Surely there couldn't be any message there for the poor. After all, they are quite familiar with poverty and stables. Would you not think the message was intended for the wealthy? Lest in their blown-up egos and high notions they may forget the reason for their sojourn on this earth. Wasn't there something in that Testament you mentioned about Man being made in God's likeness? If this is true, and after all we profess to be a Christian people, are the employers who treat their workers in that fashion not in fact locking God out of their houses at night and doing the very thing that you have mentioned? Isn't it true, the reason Christ was born in a stable, there was no room at the inn?'

51

The priest had obviously received a blow to the solar plexus that he wasn't expecting, and he now had an angry look about him. 'That may be, Pad,' he said. 'But the Devil can quote Scripture to suit himself.'

My father looked at him closely. 'I hope you're not referring to me as the Devil?' he said.

The nun now speaks for the first time. 'It's all very well for you to talk,' she said. 'The farm belongs to my brother, it's his property, what goes on there has nothing to do with us.'

Pad looked at her for a moment. 'Miss,' he said, 'when a human being is blackguarded it's everyone's business. Are you aware, that at the height of the slave trade, when it was the policy of certain governments to make full use of this free labour, that Catholic Bishops, and indeed the Catholic Church in general, when pressed by those humane countries that were throwing their weight behind the movement to abolish this barbaric practice, justified their condoning of it by stating openly that black people had no souls, and were put on earth by God for the use and benefit of the whites? Are the farming community in this country far away from that attitude in their treatment of their workers?'

The two began to walk away from the quay along the riverbank. Pad called after them. 'Do you know something?' he said. 'If Christ was born in Ireland at the present time, he'd have plenty of company in the stable, and I don't mean asses and bullocks. He'd also need to be wary of weddings where the booze was scarce – I'm telling you, they'd have him in jail for making poteen!'

The workman continued living in the barn as before, until his health could no longer withstand the cold and damp of that rat-hole, and he was of no more use to the farmer. He was taken for the first and only motorcar ride of his life, his destination, the Home in Newcastle West. He lived there for three years, and when he died, he was laid to rest in the Paupers' Plot. He had plenty of company, as most of the older farmers' boys of the area went the same road; the younger ones escaped to England. . .

Seven

Around this time, the Clareman and his employer visited a fair in Rathkeale to purchase a bull. If they were drunk when they bought him I cannot say, but they certainly arrived home with a dearie. In appearance, he was the ugliest-looking animal imaginable.

To reach the shore overland, it was necessary for us to cross this farm. From the day this animal arrived on the scene, we entered the area with extreme care. What was peculiar about him was he did not have to see you to chase you. If he should get your scent in the air, he immediately began a search to locate you. He would put his nose to the ground and trail you like a dog.

In the beginning, we felt safe behind high walls. We very soon realised that six-foot walls meant nothing to this fellow – the ones he couldn't jump, he knocked. It was only too obvious why his previous owner had given him the road. His present owners now contemplated the same solution, but there was only one problem; he couldn't be caught. When it was time to bring the cows from the fields for milking, it was necessary to travel on horseback. If he should get you in open country, you would indeed need to be fast on your kippens to make your escape.

At the time this bull was purchased, a Mission arrived in the village. The spinster sister on the farm began to prevail on the Clareman to go to confession to the Missioners. She was well aware that all the time he had been in residence at the farm he hadn't darkened the door of the Chapel. At that time, the visit of a Mission seemed to infuse the people of a parish with a great religious fervour, and finally, some of this fervour communicating itself to the workman, he took the plunge, in every sense of the word, and decided to be said by the woman of the house.

Never one to do things by half, he prepared carefully for this undertaking. He took himself to a rainwater barrel at the end of a shed,

53

and stripped to the skin and scrubbed and rubbed himself from head to toe. He then dressed himself in his best clothes and polished boots, and left for the village to perform his worthy task. He didn't go straight to the Chapel, however, but first visited a few pubs to charge his batteries. Finally he reached the Chapel and entered the box to commence his long and arduous tale for the Missioner.

When the ordeal was over, and the Clareman again got into the light of day, he could not believe that what he'd expected to be such a painful process, was in fact so simple. He became light-headed with relief, and again returned to the village to celebrate. Children he met along the way could be forgiven for thinking it was their birthday, as he plied them with sweets. He was in fact on top of the world. On his return journey along the country road leading to the farm, he knocked at doors where he had long been barred. He now wished to make peace with his neighbours, and the world in general.

During the Clareman's absence at the village, things had been happening at the farm.

One of Brody's cows decided she required the urgent amorous attention of a bull. The new arrival in the next farm decided he was the very fellow to perform this task, and without more ado knocked a huge gap in the boundary fence and commenced to satisfy Brody's cow in no uncertain manner. While the antics between bull and cow were in progress, twenty sheep belonging to Brody streamed through the gap left by the bull and thereby gained an entry to a garden of wheat which had been planted with loving care by the Clareman. The sheep now began to eat their fill of the crop and trample the remainder into the ground.

Into the middle of this situation strolled the happy penitent on his way back from the village. For a moment, his eyes could not take in the full significance of the scene; then he began bellowing like a man possessed. Froth poured from his mouth, and he tore across the wheat field and jumped onto the boundary wall of Brody's yard. The Spanker was in the process of washing milk cans, in preparation for the evening milking. When he saw the Clareman standing on the wall, waving his clenched fists at the sky, and roaring like a madman, he decided that to vacate the yard in a hurry might be a good idea, and he bolted towards the haybarn. He hadn't gone far however, when a blow of a rock between the shoulder blades knocked him kicking to the ground.

Liza Brody, having been attracted from the kitchen by the bellowing Clareman, ran towards the little spailpeen to render assistance. The

"The new arrival in the next farm decided he was
the very fellow to perform this task...."

Clareman sucked her into his bellicose vocabulary in an instant. 'Oh Jasus,' he roared, 'look who's coming now, with her long ass's ear of a nose.'

Jim Brody's uncle was sitting peacefully in the kitchen reading a newspaper. Hearing the thunderous voice of the workman, and at the same instant looking through the front window, saw the bull performing for all he was worth, decided this was the root of the Clareman's anger. He whistled two sheepdogs from under the kitchen table, and opening the front door, set them at the visiting bull. The animal didn't seem in the least pleased at this interruption in his urgent task; however, he was forced to retreat back through the breach in the boundary wall, and made off across the field bucking and roaring, with the two sheepdogs still showing him the way.

The Clareman, seeing the bull emerging from the field, and now assuming they had had a service free gratis, on top of everything else, commenced to roar louder than ever, and began to shout the Brody pedigree to the high heavens, at least as much of it as his employers had been able to pass on to him.

The elder bachelor brother and his sister were standing at their kitchen door, listening to the sound of their employee's voice echoing over the fields, tearing strips off their neighbours, when the bull came pounding into the yard with Brody's two sheepdogs snapping at his heels. The dogs, having completed their task, turned tail and fled back across the field. The bull charged on, to the huge wooden trough that stood under the pump at the corner of the yard. He pushed his head into the water and began to drink greedily; obviously he was thirsty from his recent exertions.

The little bachelor decided that, once and for all, something must be done about this animal. When they had purchased him, a ring had already been fitted to his nose, and the farmer was now regretting his folly in not having secured a good heavy chain to this ring, while they still had him in captivity. However, better late than never, and he resolved to make another effort now to capture him while he was at the water trough. He went back into the kitchen; from the thatch over the door he pulled a reaping hook, and then crossed the yard towards the pump.

As the farmer approached, the bull wheeled suddenly, and began lashing the air with his tail. He would then advance a step or two, and retreat again, all the time making a strange rumbling sound deep in his throat. The farmer continued on towards him, holding the hook with the point of the blade turned upwards. 'Easy boy,' he said, 'easy boy.' The bull shook his head and snorted, took a step forward, then back again. The farmer was close enough.

He struck upwards with the hook, driving the point into the ring on the animal's nose. For a moment the bull stood rock-still, then, with a flick of his head, he pitched the farmer backwards onto the cobbled yard as if he had been a rag doll. Then he rushed to where the man was lying on his back, knelt his front legs over his chest, and began pounding him to pulp with his head.

To the north of this farm was the shooting ground I've already mentioned called Shanna Walla. The region was completely covered with furze and ferns, and was a haunt of woodcock and pheasants. The marsh stretching between this area and the river had many freshwater springs, beloved of woodcock. In the middle of this was in residence a cock pheasant that had become the plague of our lives. Hell or the devil could not compel him to take to the air. Now and then you could see flashes of his beautiful colours, as he slipped through the cover, but take to the air, he just would not do.

On this particular evening, we had come to make an all-out effort to drive him into the open and do him in.

There is only one dog to drive a pheasant from cover that doesn't want to be driven, 'a fistful of a fox terrier'. We had been given a present of just such an animal some time previously. For some strange reason he had been called 'Lonesome'. There certainly wasn't anything lonesome about him. We didn't have him in our possession long when it became obvious why we had been presented with him so conveniently. His speciality was hiding inside the road gate, to watch for any pony and cart or donkey and cart that might pass on its way to the creamery. He would then streak after the cart, rush in between the wheels and sink his teeth in the leg of the unfortunate animal. The driver would have no inkling of what was going on until the animal made a rush to escape. Never once was he heard to bark.

We were now busy with Lonesome and Fly, attempting to drive this rogue of a pheasant from the furze, when suddenly, over the fields came a piercing howling wail that turned my blood to water. Pad looked at me from the other side of a clump of furze. 'In the name of Jesus,' he said, 'what was that?'

Before I could reply, the sound came again. Fly and Lonesome had stopped dead in their tracks and were listening too. Flocks of redshank and green plover that were feeding along the estuary sloblands took to the air and flew wildly away to the north. Then the sound came again. Could it have come from a human throat? Surely only a soul in mortal agony could utter such an unearthly call. It was the sound of a man screaming. Then, almost immediately, a woman's screams intermingled with it, and a strange symphony of sound began to echo and re-echo along the Deel Estuary.

Before it died away, Pad was moving fast towards the source of those tortured anguished cries. Over his shoulder he shouted, 'Come on, Jesus, come on.'

I was close on his heels when he vaulted the wall into the yard where the bull had been about his gruesome work. He was now pawing the ground and making darts at a whitethorn bush growing near the pump. This bush had saved the life of the little spinster. When he had tired of his attack on the farmer, the bull turned his attention to her. She had made a valiant effort to save her brother. While the blood-crazed animal was tearing him to pieces, she grabbed a pail off the stand near the door and running to the trough, slashed pail after pail of water into the bull's face. He abandoned the farmer and charged her. Whether by luck or fair shooting she sidestepped him, and he merely brushed her with his shoulder. The force was sufficient however to send her flying into this bush. When next he charged, the thorns and branches checked his advance.

As we entered the yard from the north, the Clareman came running in on the same track taken by the bull a short while before. The screams had reached his ears in spite of the noise he was making himself. He was closely followed by the Spanker and the woman he referred to as having the 'long ass's ear of a nose'. Several other members of the Brody family, including Jim, were sprinting across the field towards the yard of death.

The bull, finding himself surrounded, spun round on his hind legs, the reaping-hook, now covered in blood and pieces of cloth, still hanging from his nose. His eyes focused on the Clareman, and he charged at once. The workman took to his heels across the yard with the bull in pursuit, but the hook seemed to hamper his movements, and the Clareman reached the pump and ducked around it, all the time shouting, 'Jasus, Pad, shoot him, will you, shoot him, will you!'

It is not as simple as one might think, to shoot an animal running close on the heels of someone, intent on doing that person a mischief. Pad now began to shout at the Clareman, 'Run to me, run to me.' Finally the Clareman got the message, and left the comparative safety of the pump and streaked across the yard. As he was passing, Pad already had a gun to his shoulder with a three-inch cartridge in the breech.

The blast struck the bull just above the eyes and took off the top of his head; he turned cartwheel, his back legs striking a wooden garden seat and sending it flying; when his body struck the ground it gave a great shiver and lay still. A deathly silence settled over the homestead and surrounding fields. We stood in different positions round the yard, then a sob, coming from the bush near the pump, brought us back to reality and we all reacted together. Some ran to help the little woman from the bush; she had been lucky to escape with just a few scratches on her hands and face. Jim Brody and I were drawn to the heap of blood-stained clothing and battered flesh. A messenger was dispatched to the village for a doctor and priest, but one did not need a doctor to know that the farmer was long past help of any kind.

The farmer's remains were lifted gently by these rough workers of the land, and borne into the thatched farmhouse and placed on his bed. When his clothes were removed, it was obvious what had caused most of those terrible wounds. The reaping hook, locked in the bull's nose, and dragged backwards and forwards during his frenzied attack, acted as the blade on a bacon-slicer.

The Clareman was standing in the middle of the kitchen looking strangely out of place in his 'good clothes' and blood-stained polished boots. His cap was discarded, and he was running his fists across the bald patch on top of his head. The effects of the porter he had consumed in the village had been quickly neutralised.

The little spinster sister was going round the kitchen picking up the clothes that were soaked in blood and water and putting them to dry across a chair near the fire. The fact that her brother would not need clothing again in this life had not yet penetrated her benumbed brain.

The second bachelor brother, with the strange little pointed face like a polecat ferret, and the boots that seemed to be forever turned up at the toes like a wizard's, had also come in from the fields. He slipped into his room and came out again carrying a bottle of whiskey. He sat on a settle bed at the side of the kitchen and began taking great gulps of the fiery liquid direct from the bottle. He hadn't spoken a word to anyone, 'he rarely spoke anyhow'.

Suddenly the Clareman gave a shout. ''Tis all your fault,' he said, addressing the sister. 'If it wasn't for you and your confession I'd have been here to save him.' The little woman's only reply was to put her apron over her face and commence to weep hysterically. Pad put his hand on the workman's shoulder and said, 'Take it easy, take it easy.'

The Clareman was beside himself with emotion. 'What will I do at all?' he said. 'What will I do at all?' He was weeping wildly.

It was strange the affection he had for his employers. It was as if he had adopted them body and soul as his own family. It is a positive fact that he had often taken the farmer that was now lying dead in the room, and, putting him across his knee, beaten him soundly on the backside as if he was a bold child, and on more than one occasion had used a stick for this purpose.

He was pacing wildly across the kitchen, suddenly he stopped near Pad, and through his tears shouted, 'Will you shave him?'

To me, standing near the door close to Jim Brody and holding tightly to my muzzle-loader, the remark seemed to break the spell that had settled over that homestead after the horrific experience. The remainder of those present seemed to relax a little too, and began to whisper to each other about things that had no bearing whatever on the present circumstances. It was a routine as old as time. That simple remark from the Clareman was the call of life itself, picking up its skirts and again rushing onwards, bearing us forward, in its relentless journey through time and space.

Eight

The house now took on a hustle and bustle as everyone tried to help. A plan of campaign was drawn up with each being allotted his or her task. The Clareman and Pad went to the yard and removed the heavy wooden door from the barn and brought it into the kitchen where it was placed on several barrels. This would become the bier, but first it would become the wash-stand for the body of the dead. They went to the room and brought the corpse, completely naked, and placed it on this. It was black as tar.

Jim Brody's aunt ushered myself and Jim out to the yard and began to prepare a list for us to take to the village. On the way we will inform two old women living in a thatched cottage that their services are required to put the finishing touches to the 'laying-out'.

Jim Brody and I must first perform a hazardous task. We must tackle a pony, owned by these people, to the common cart. This pony was called The Gypsy. The Clareman had aptly named her. When just a little foal, he had purchased her from a family of tinkers, camped near the village. Apart from the bull, whose remains were lying in the yard waiting for the knacker's cart, God had rarely put a more cantankerous animal on the face of the earth as this pony. Her eyes were almost completely white. If you should see one of those eyes gazing backwards over the winkers, you must take great care, lest you recieve a lash of a steel-shod hoof. The Clareman loved her dearly, and the feeling was mutual. Anyone else coming within range of her feet or head was taking his or her life in their hands. It wasn't that she'd let fly with one leg, she could use all four together.

We finally had her between the shafts of the car, with Jim in charge of the reins. She also had the nasty habit, when approaching a gate, of making a mad rush and crashing the cart into the pier. This she now proceeds to do, in spite of all Jim's pulling on the rope. I now twist Jim's tail by telling him he knows nothing about controlling 'spirited animals', being only accustomed to the 'H.O.R.S.E. horse grey mare'. Jim gets red in the face and hits The Gypsy a swipe of the reins. She in turn kicks the two centre boards of the cart to smithereens, and so we proceed towards the village.

We enter a pub-cum-grocery at the corner, and hand in our list: two barrels of porter, several bottles of whiskey, wines of all sorts, tobacco, wax candles, crates of lemonade, biscuits, sweets – 'whatever this wake will be short of, it won't be biscuits or lemonade'. We load the lot into the cart. Jim runs to a butcher's stall across the road for a leg of mutton. The cart is full to overflowing, all very well if we can get back to the farm without The Gypsy making dust of the lot.

When we arrive back in the yard, with just a few minor kicks and screeches from The Gypsy, more neighbours have arrived and the house is beginning to fill up. The bier in the kitchen is now covered with a white sheet and the corpse is laid out in one of those abominable brown dresses called a 'habit'.

For many years, three of these 'habits' had been stored in a cupboard in one of the bedrooms, and were taken out periodically and aired. It was widely believed at the time that the keeping of these death clothes in the house gained numerous indulgences for their owners, or 'intended owners'.

The barrels of porter were lifted with extreme care from the cart and rolled into the kitchen where they were placed on a block of wood. The two brass taps and wooden mallet supplied by the publican were handed to a neighbour to do the tapping. According to himself he had performed this task thousands of times during his world-wide travels, and on one occasion was obliged to display his talent 'for royalty'. He was told however, in words he could plainly understand, that if he was to make a mess of the present operation, his travels in future would be limited, to say the least. True to his word, he performed flawlessly, and soon the porter was flowing freely.

As time passed, and more and more containers of the black fluid were poured down gullets, and more and more neighbours arrived, someone suggested it was time to think about food. The fellow that had appointed himself master of ceremonies decided to 'put on' the leg of mutton we had brought from the village. The huge black cooking-pot was hung on the pothooks hanging from the crane over the fire of sticks and turf; the leg of mutton, a bucket of spring water, and a fistful of salt went into this, and that was it, there were no further embellishments.

The two old ladies that had come to lay out the corpse were sitting well in near the fire and downing mugs of porter as fast as anyone else and getting very talkative, as were all the rest of the gathering. A wizened little man sitting on a sugain chair near the door and leaning one hand on a stout walking-stick, made himself heard.

'Did I ever tell ye about the blackguard of a rat that tormented myself and my oul woman for years? Every time we put down a clutch of duck eggs or hen eggs this bastard of a rat was sure to get into the house and destroy them. I put down a trap every night with the bait securely tied, but sure enough, in the morning the trap was snapped and the bait gone. Myself and the oul woman sat up all night to see how he managed it. In the quiet of the morning on he came, as big as a badger, the Lord save us, such a rat you never saw. When he thought he had the place to himself, he examined the trap carefully. He then ran to a pile of sticks in the corner of the yard, selected one that suited his needs, brought it back across the yard in his mouth and snapped the trap without any danger to himself.'

With the conclusion of this story, every man and woman sitting around the kitchen was anxious to get in with their own tales.

It is said that the Irish were once the greatest story-tellers in the world. This may or may not be true, but certainly, if there were prizes for telling lies, they would be high on the list of winners. Being good liars is a gift that seems to have been bestowed on the Irish in great abundance. The crowd gathered in that kitchen were well endowed with this gift.

There now followed some of the most outrageous lies and tall yarns imaginable. The master of ceremonies was already off with his own rat story. This rat was not as big in stature as the last one, but he was lacking nothing in cunning. This rat was in residence in the story-teller's orchard, and each morning he climbed into an apple tree, and moving carefully along a branch he would bite into one apple after another until he found what he was looking for. 'And what was that?' one of the old ladies in the corner wanted to know. There was a chorus of voices from the background: 'a sweet one, of course'.

The Clareman is now relating a tale of an adventure that befell himself and his brother, many years before in the city of Liverpool. It is obvious that during our absence in the village, the Clareman and Pad did not confine their activities to just shaving the dead farmer. They had observed the other brother visiting the room and returning with the whiskey. As soon as they got at the 'blind side' of this little man they slipped into the room and robbed his nest.

The Clareman continues, 'When we landed in Liverpool we were broke to the ropes. We saw a sign over a pub door: *All-in Wrestling Tonight, Challengers Welcome, Prizes To Be Won.* Well, I'm telling you, the brother was the man for this job, he was twice the size of me. When we got to the bar, there was a fellow going round offering a pound note to anyone that would stay in the ring with this big Chinese for one round. Before he was finished, the brother was inside the ring they had rigged up in the centre of the pub, and in a few seconds he got to grips with this Chinaman. They pulled and dragged, and then they both fell to the floor completely tied in a knot, neither one of them able to move an inch. And then, blasht me, didn't the brother see a big pair of balls, and blasht me, didn't he make a snap at them with his teeth, and blasht me, weren't they his own.'

The stories continued into the night. It was as if the assembled neighbours were prepared to relate and listen to any tale, no matter how preposterous, in an effort to guide the mind away from the stark reality of the mutilated body lying so still on top of the barn door.

The black pot over the fire was beginning to give off a beautiful smell of cooking meat. Whenever the cover was removed to inspect the contents, penknives were surreptitiously sneaked from pockets and chunks of the half-cooked meat hacked off, and devoured immediately, lest the eagle-eye of the master of ceremonies observe this uncouth practice. The fact that the meat was only partially cooked, didn't matter in the least to people whose appetites had received a sharp edge from an over-abundance of porter. When the meat was to be 'officially' removed from the pot, in the small hours of the morning, all that remained was the bone, well and truly picked clean.

When the meat was found to be finished, the gathering hit on a second-best procedure, and commenced filling their mugs with the water left in the black pot. This 'soup' was given a wide berth by Pad and me; we had been burned too often by the goose soup, with the resulting consequences. The drinking of this water had a devastating effect on the assembly, and soon, first one, and then another, until the kitchen was almost empty, the neighbours took to the fields, and for a long time that night, their moans and groans could be heard coming from under hedges and ditches, as the incompatible mixture of porter and mutton soup fought each other in a mad rush to escape.

When the wake had been officially begun by the master of ceremonies, his first task was to stop the clock. This practice was widespread at the time, and is in fact not as simple as one might think.

There were several experts present, who according to themselves were old hands at this, but try as they might, the little alarm clock ticked on, until finally it was taken to an outside shed to wind itself out.

As the night dragged on, and the assembly was beginning to get back to some normality after the recent visits to the outdoors, one of the old ladies in the corner threw back her head and released the strangest cry I've ever heard since or before. The other old woman immediately took it up, but in a lower key. The first woman then stopped, and the second moved to the higher pitch, then the other began again lower down the scale. For a moment I thought they were singing, but no song ever sounded like that, neither was it crying. It was a strange and disturbing mournful wail.

I moved in closer to where Pad was sitting and gave him a nudge. 'What's wrong with them?' I asked. He turned and smiled at me. 'Don't take any notice of them,' he said, 'they're full of porter.' 'I know that,' I replied, 'but why are they making that noise?' 'Oh, that,' he said, 'they're only keening.'

Of all the customs ever practised at wakes and funerals in Ireland, surely this one of keening was the strangest. It was also used by the American Red Indian. In modern-day jargon it would probably be called 'rent a mourner'. Men could not make a fist of it. One needed the larynx of the female to reach the high-pitched wail required.

The payment for this performance was a plentiful supply of porter (one needed this to lubricate the machinery and induce the correct state of melancholy) and 'the dead plucks'. These were the clothes of the dead. If the relatives wished to make a good impression, it was the practice to purchase new clothing to give to the keener. The employing of the keener and giving away of the dead plucks was supposed to hurry the soul of the departed on its flight through space to its heavenly home.

Towards nightfall, the hearse that would bear away the mortal remains of the dead farmer arrived in the yard. It was a magnificent sight, silver-mounted and drawn by two matching black horses with plumes on their heads. The brown box was removed from the inside of this weird and beautiful death car and taken into the kitchen; moments later it was again seen coming through the doorway and was replaced in the berth behind the driver of those two beautiful beasts. A flick of the whip, and the remains were borne away, never to be seen again by human eyes . . .

Nine

We are making another assault on the cock pheasant that has made the furze of Shanna Walla his abode. Lonesome is hot on his heels, tearing through these thorny brambles, with Fly keeping a watchful eye on the open spaces. We have had lightning glimpses of this extraordinary bird, as he again performs his cunning manoeuvres to outsmart us. A flurry of wings overhead makes us both look up and the most magnificent creature we have ever seen streaks past, emitting a call very similar to that of a gander. But this was no gander. The colouring on his feathers seemed like those of the rainbow, while his legs appeared to trail behind him like the steering oar on a boat. His strange call echoed several times, and then he dropped onto the marsh. When he touched the ground he was running, and he seemed to cover the grass like the boy in the seven-league boots Old Rooney had so often told us about in school. When he came to a stop, he stretched to his full height and opened his wings. From head to toe he must be four or five feet high.

Pad is already moving towards the marsh to get a closer look. The creature doesn't seem at all wild. We in fact got as close as twenty yards without it showing any sign of concern, and we were so taken with its beautiful colouring and strange antics, that neither one of us thought to put a gun to the shoulder and bowl him over.

He would dip his head into a flash of water on the marsh, in what appeared to us an upside down position and drag it to and fro; we had never seen the like before. We were so taken with this, that we didn't notice Fly creeping forward and making a sudden rush at the visitor. He in turn gave a mighty leap into the air flapping his wings wildly, released a few loud gander screeches and took off for the White Island.

Pad whipped off his cap and lashed it off the ground. 'Well God blast you, Fly,' he said, 'and it's not the first time you've done it to me. Come on,' he said, 'we'll follow him.' The White Island at that time was not an island in the true sense of the word. Its owner had had two banks of mud and stones built across the intervening mud basin which stretched between the island and the mainland thereby gaining himself some extra land (I might add that the tide succeeded in taking it back shortly afterwards). The strange visitor had landed in a pond of water on the island and was out of range of any cover.

We now decided to work an old trick we had used many times to shoot wild geese. The piece of string was securely tied round Fly's neck lest he get any more notions of capturing this stranger all by himself, Lonesome was given a hard kick which brought him to heel in a hurry, and we moved on out the bank towards our quarry. I now circle around the island, keeping well out of sight, and then return in a direct line from the opposite shore, in an attempt to drive the stranger over the tidal bank where Pad was lying in wait.

It worked like a charm. The creature took to the air and streaked towards the bank in that strange extended flight position. Suddenly, he stalled, and staggered, and was already falling to earth when I heard the report of the shot. We stood and gazed at this magnificent bird for a long time. We turned and twisted him this way and that, trying to figure out what he might be. It was his beak that really puzzled us, it seemed twisted upside down.

When we reached home the people there were as mystified as ourselves. Pad had come to a decision: he would take the bird to his friend in the city that owned the only sports-shop there at that time, and was an expert in the art of taxidermy. On his journey there the following day he had occasion to visit the Post Office in the village.

The Post-Mistress, who had been 'away' at school for some time and was looked on as an intellectual in the area, put her eye on the strange bird. 'Wherever did you get that?' she inquired. 'Down at the shore,' Pad told her, 'but I haven't a clue what it is.' The lady came from behind the counter and examined the bird carefully. 'Well,' she said, 'I just don't know what's wrong with ye around here; couldn't any fool see, that's a young ostrich.'

The bird was taken to the city and delivered to the sports store. Its identity as just as big a mystery there. One thing everyone was agreed on, it certainly was not a young ostrich. The store owner prevailed on Pad to allow the strange bird to remain in his shop (he's standing proudly there to this day). Twelve months later, an English visitor went to the store to purchase cartridges. Walking round the shop, looking with interest on the many curios, he came on the beautiful bird with the twisted beak. 'In Heaven's name,' he said aloud, 'where did ye get the flamingo?'

" He would dip his head into a flash of water ...
and drag it backwards and forwards .."

Ten

'What's the capital of France?' Old Rooney has a firm grip on a boy's ear, keeping his face turned towards the window as if he might see the answer in the green fields that stretched away to the southern horizon. Rooney is making sure the unfortunate lad will not get a prompt from some boy with a better knowledge of geography than himself. 'Do you know?' he shouts at him again. The lad twists and turns in an effort to extricate his ear from the Master's fingers, but finally has to admit defeat. 'No, sir,' he sobs. Surprisingly, the Master releases the boy's ear and walks to his usual place at the window. He gazes out for some time, then mutters under his breath, 'God knows, if the truth was told, maybe you're as well off.'

Jim Brody and I are looking forward to the final lessons. We have been laying our plans carefully for some time. Near the ruined Abbey on the banks of the River Deel is a magnificent pear tree loaded down with that beautiful fruit that is just now about ready for a visit from two boys with a fair-sized sack. After school, this sack is collected from a bush behind the boundary wall and we're off across Tom Charley's Hill on our way to the river. The tide is out; as I've said, we have been laying our plans for some time.

The reason this pear tree escapes the attentions of other boys in the area is no accident. The owner of the land adjacent to the Abbey, where this tree is growing, is a force to be reckoned with. He's a man in his mid-seventies, but is still hale and hearty. He's also cunning as a fox, and seems to know all the tricks and moves of young boys that are intent on transferring fruit from one owner to another. Last, but by no means least, 'he also has a stout blackthorn stick'. It has become a battle of wills between him and us, and this evening we're going to put our plan to the test and dare the Devil in his den.

On our way to the tree we must take great care not to walk into an ambush. We cross the river near the Abbey and enter the outside burial ground. We'll survey the countryside from here. The advantage of this approach from the west may benefit us; it must surely give us the element of surprise. The old farmer will not expect an attack from this direction through the river.

We have the tree with its golden hoard under observation. All looks peaceful. 'Come on, Jim, it's now or never.' We vault the boundary wall (that in the past had been the cause of such dissension in the village) and rush across the open space for the tree. Jim will climb into the branches as fast as possible and shake the fruit to the ground, while I will throw it into the sack, all the time keeping a weather eye open for the farmer with the blackthorn stick.

Speed is of the essence and we are soon bounding back for the Abbey and tumble headlong over the wall into the graveyard, with our hearts in our mouths, as if all the devils in Hell were on our heels. We listen, there is no sound of running feet or shouted anger, all is very still. We sit under the wall, with the afternoon sun streaming into that peaceful setting. Then we begin to laugh. The more the tension-taut nerves relaxed the more we laughed and giggled, until suddenly, the thought of our surroundings brought us up short and we grew silent again.

So we had pulled it off. It was strange, but now that we had actually done the deed, the fruit no longer looked as attractive. Somehow, looking at it in the distance, growing on the tree, it appeared more yellow in colour, and in our imaginations we had been able to feel our fingers sinking into its luscious flesh, while now Jim Brody is grousing and has the cheek to say they're 'hard as rocks'.

'Listen,' I say, 'while we're here, will we have a look at the little black man?' Jim grudgingly condescends.

We enter the darker confines of the ruin and make our way to the image of the little black figure carved on the wall. Its surface is smooth as a bottle. This condition was brought about from every shape and type of mouth tonguing and kissing it down through the years.

This little statue contained strong magic. It could cure the most vicious toothache. To perform this miracle, you first kissed the statue three times, then you spun around twice on your left heel and again kissed it three times. You performed this routine for a total of nine, and then the toothache just drifted away. On the floor under the little stone image a hole had been gouged out from the constant friction of many heels.

It is a fact that certain individuals from the village had left their beds on many a night, and, overcoming the strange and quite unnatural fear the Irish have of the dead, directed their steps to this spot in a last hope that this ritual would in some way ease the pain that was driving them insane. Strange to say, it worked for many of them. Others, probably having added to their suffering by allowing the cold night air to come in contact with a throbbing molar, left the Abbey in a worse condition than when they arrived, roundly cursing little black men, and in particular, little black Spaniards, as this one was reputed to be.

He was a Prince of that country, so our story goes. Wealth and power were his in abundance. He had a daughter, whose beauty was outstanding, even for a country so rich in beautiful women. The girl, having finished school, had just returned to her father's house from the convent, where she had been taught everything about life, except the most important – 'how to protect herself from the pitfalls of the world'. A party was arranged in her honour, and in the evening it was suggested that a boat-trip on the river would be just the thing to finish off the day. The father owned a river boat, and the boy that took care of it, a lad just in his late teens, had been left as a baby on the Prince's doorstep and reared in the household until such time it was agreed by the Prince he should help the ageing boatman on the river.

The daughter, being of royal birth, was not allowed the freedom of ordinary children, and although she was aware of the presence of this boy in her father's household, they had never actually met face to face.

When the party arrrived at the river bank and were picking their steps into the boat, the two teenagers looked into each other's eyes for the first time. What followed was to tear that family asunder, and, in the end, land the Prince a penniless pauper in the West Limerick village where his bones are now in dust.

The look exchanged by the teenagers sent a pang of ecstatic pain through their hearts. The girl had no longer any interest in the journey down-river. She could not take her eyes off the dark-haired boy so expertly handling the tiller. The glances exchanged between the pair escaped all, except the eagle eye of the girl's mother. She made no comment, but a cold and heavy weight seemed to settle on her heart. That night, when the household grew quiet with sleep, the daughter was glimpsed fleetingly as she sped on bare feet towards the river. Behind the slatted window the hand of fear gripped tighter round the heart of the mother. Sleep had deserted her. All the afternoon and into the night the image of the look exchanged between the boy and her daughter remained before her eyes. She could not understand the unreasoning fear it had brought to her being.

Night after night she would keep her vigil at the window. She was caught in a quandary. If she was to tell her husband, knowing his violent temper, the danger to her daughter and the boy in the boat was great. The same boy she had watched from a distance as he grew to manhood, wishing he was the son she never had. If she should broach the subject direct with her daughter, would the consequences be the same?

The matter, however, was taken out of her hands. At nine o'clock in the morning the housemaid knocked on her door; she was distressed. She had tried in vain to locate the daughter, but she was nowhere to be found. The mother, realising the folly of her actions, called her husband and broke the news. The Prince made no comment. He called a servant from the kitchen and bade him fetch the boy. The servant was back shortly with the news that the boy was gone. The Prince went to the hall and buckled on his sword. The search commenced.

With his wealth and influence it did not take long to run them to earth. The bedroom door of the shabby lodging-house where they had taken shelter was kicked in. The noise brought the lovers from their sleep in a hurry. They were as yet unable to appreciate their danger. The boy, attempting to rise from the bed, was decapitated by a lash of the father's sword. The daughter, rushing to help her fallen lover, was run through with the same sword.

As she fell dying on the bed, she whispered, 'Father, we were married. You've killed your grandchild too.'

The Prince, like all hotheads when the deed was done, was insane with remorse and grief. He threw down his sword and ran from the house, weeping wildly. His ensuing mad rush through the streets of the town led him, whether by fate or accident, to the door of a monastery where he collapsed. The early-rising monks, on their way into the town to render assistance to the poor, found this richly-clad man still unconscious. They carried him bodily into the chamber where the Abbot was at morning prayer.

The Prince finally awoke to the nightmare of reality which was more unbearable than that which had haunted him during his shock-induced sleep. He began to relate the gruesome story to the old monk. When he was finished, the old man remained silent for a long time, then he spoke. His words hammered into the Prince's brain like the voice of doom.

'There is no forgiveness for the crime you have committed,' he said. 'You must take yourself away from the fair land of Spain and never look upon her mountains and valleys again. You will wander the world with the mark of Cain upon your head, until in your closing days you will come into the Land of Gurt, and there end your life's span begging God's mercy.'

So, the Prince took to the highways and byways of Europe, moving ever onwards in search of the place called Gurt, until finally he landed on the green shores of Hibernia and bent his weary footsteps towards the Atlantic Seaboard. He arrived in the village on the Deel Estuary at nightfall in the springtime of the year. He turned north into the lane that ran beside the river. He was no longer to be recognised as the proud Prince that had left Spain so many years before. His clothes were in tatters, and he was footsore and heart-scalded. He sat himself on a grassy bank at the roadside and listened to the sound of children playing in the distance. It brought back the vision of his garden in Spain and from the house ran his beautiful daughter calling his name. He could see her clearly. He fought hard to retain her image; it helped to ease the terrible pain that was eating at his insides since that awful night in the boarding-house.

A woman in one of the little thatched cabins in the lane stuck her head over a halfdoor and shouted into the twilight, 'Kieran, Kieran.'

From a distance a boy's voice answered, 'What's up, ma?'

The woman shouted again. 'Run down to Gurt Na Siugra for the goats before it gets dark.'

The pilgrim was still trying hard to retain the vision in his mind's eye, but some part of his brain had picked up the woman's words and was even now busily digesting them. The picture faded from his mind and he struggled painfully to his feet. He moved slowly towards the door where the woman was standing. As he drew near she called to him, 'I've nothing for you, I'm looking for help myself.'

The pilgrim drew closer. 'Please, madam,' he said, 'I only wanted to ask you what you shouted at the boy.'

'Yerrah,' she said, 'I only asked him to run for the goats.'

The traveller looked at her closely. 'Madam,' he said, 'did you mention the word "Gurt"?'

'I did, of course,' she replied. 'Isn't that where the goats are?'

Her reply had an effect on the old man that the woman was not expecting; he fell to his knees and tears streamed down his dust-stained face. 'Thank God,' he said. 'My journey is over, thank God.'

The pilgrim set up home on the bank of the river on the brow of a limestone hill. He spent most of his waking hours working amongst the poor of the locality, and very soon became known as the pilgrim healer. His fame spread far and wide, and the people flocked from the surrounding countryside to visit the strange hermit that was reputed to have such miraculous healing powers. An order of monks arrived at the village to expose this charlatan: they stayed to build an Abbey around his little home.

Before he died, he asked that no marker should point out his grave, but some time after his death a young monk stone-cutter carved out the little black statue and placed it on the pillar of the nave. Beside it was the inscription, *Pass Me By, I Am A Stranger.*

Eleven

The Abbey was built on the side of a limestone hill. The monks then set about filling in the area in front of the building which was washed by the River Deel. This reclaimed area would become the courtyard, and in later years became what was known as the outside burial ground. It was obviously never intended for this purpose. When the tide was full, the water penetrated from underneath, and if a grave should be open at this time, it was necessary for the mourners to weight down the coffin with stones. As one distraught parent would put it, having seen the coffin containing the remains of his baby daughter so treated, 'It isn't fair to the little human body.'

The boundary wall between this graveyard and the adjoining farm is believed by many to be an original part of the Abbey buildings; this is not so. The wall was erected after an event in the not-so-distant past, an event which even now, at this distance in time, seems incredible. The boundary fence at the time was a shambles. The farmer, from whom we have just gone to such lengths to remove the fruit of his pear treee, had purchased a massive breeding sow, and she had been released into the field beside the Abbey.

Two days previously, two sisters from the village had been taken from this life by what was called at the time, 'the decline' (we know it now as tuberculosis). Only hours separated their deaths, and they were laid to rest side by side in the outside burial ground just a short time before the sow's release in the adjoining field. During the hours of darkness, this huge creature with the insatiable appetite of her breed crashed through the makeshift fence into the graveyard. The freshly-turned earth very soon attracted the marauding sow and she began to use her powerful head to throw the soil and stones aside, her curiousity growing all the time as to the nature of what lay hidden there. She soon reached the coffins, and in minutes had smashed through the covers and dragged the two female corpses out onto the grass and tore them limb from limb.

A sow is an opportunist meat-eater. They have on many occasions dragged babies from prams and cradles in farmers' yards and devoured them. In the farm mentioned previously, where the bull had performed his dastardly deed, I personally witnessed the actions of a breeding sow when she discovered the carcase of a dead donkey. In two days she had completely devoured it. They will also of course eat their own young, given half a chance.

The animal in the graveyard, having satisfied her appetite temporarily, slipped back through the fence and found a sheltered nook to sleep off her recent indulgence. Towards morning, the wind having shifted into the north, the scent of decaying flesh reached the half-starved mongrel curs of the village, and they began to move in ones and twos towards the Abbey.

In nooks and corners, and even in kitchens and bedrooms where these curs could doubtfully claim a home base, a strange smell pervaded the air throughout the following day. It was the stomach-churning scent of half-rotten, half-digested human flesh, discharged from the crops of dogs, unable to contain this sudden abundance after lifetimes of meagreness.

The owner of the sow, unable to locate her the following day, arrived at the boundary fence and could hardly take in the scene before his eyes. The animal was savaging the remains of the bodies that had escaped the attentions of the village dogs. The bones of the two women were replaced in the grave, and the sow transferred to another area of the farm where she could not again indulge in her nightly escapades.

Shortly thereafter, a strange sickness struck down several families in the village. The water from the pump at the eastern end of the street was immediately suspect. This pump was situated in a place known in local jargon as the Latogue. An elder of the area explained that the stream feeding this spring flowed underground through another graveyard, known as the Protestant Churchyard. The pump was closed to further use. How the old man could ascertain where the stream was flowing under the village is still a mystery, but he was very close to the truth. It was not the water from the pump that caused the trouble, but the fever-laden flesh deposited round the village by the dogs.

The local medical doctor, having become aware of the true nature of the sickness, was outraged. He visited the owner of the man-eater.

77

" She found a sheltered nook to sleep off her
recent indulgence.... »

This farmer was by nature a headstrong, peevish man. When he was hot on the heels of trespassers, and the pursued was faster on his kippens than the pursuer, he would shout after his escaping quarry, 'You bastard, next time I'll shoot you with pig's blood and red pepper.'

He refused point-blank to accept the peaceful suggestion put forward by the doctor, that he should be responsible for the erection of a proper fence around the graveyard. With his continued belligerence towards the doctor, the latter threatened to expose to the people of the village the real reason for the recent outbreak of sickness. The farmer refused to budge, and the doctor, true to his word, contacted the authorities. The resulting row between government and villagers split the community into two camps.

The authorities' first reaction was to build a proper fence. Then an order was issued, 'no more burials would be allowed at the Abbey'. A local handyman was employed to construct a timber gate, and with this in position and firmly locked, the Abbey was barred to the public.

In the middle of this upheaval my grandfather died. The Abbey was the family burial-ground, and it was decided he would be laid to rest with his ancestors. The authorities refused permission, and a state of siege ensued. It was conveyed to the locals that if they were to persist in their attitude, and bury the body illegally, it would be exhumed and left by the roadside. It was decided to perform the deed under cover of darkness. In the midst of all man's arrogance and stupidity, one can find a tinge of comedy. The handyman who had gone to such pains to construct such a stout and robust door, which he hoped would remain a memorial to his craftmanship, long after his own demise, now became the leading spokesman for its removal, and was in fact the one to break it down on the fateful night.

The coffin containing my grandfather's remains was taken from the earth next day and left by the roadside. It was in fact buried and taken up again on three occasions; to this day, I have no idea which part of the Abbey holds his bones. The arrests and trials of the people involved in these goings-on reached such a degree that the authorities decided enough was enough, and the Abbey was again thrown open to the public.

Twelve

We are waiting for the evening flight at the 'back butts'. These are two stone hides Pad and I have succeeded in building on this slobland of the Long Mud. It is a fantastic stand for wildfowl, and in its day was reputed by those that should know as the best in Europe.

Tonight, however, we are waiting for a visit of the wild geese, but so far they have failed to put in an appearance. We are accompanied by two visitors, one from the village, the other from the southern end of the county. This second man is a terrific wildfowler, and indeed a wonderful character in every way, except for one thing: he has not the slightest regard for law or order. The legal shooting of wildfowl, and game in general, holds no interest for him. He must be for ever in pursuit of the forbidden fruit, and has in fact made the work of gamekeepers and gun-clubs much more difficult than it was ever intended to be.

If you were to spend too much time in this man's company, you might very soon find yourself at the wrong side of a jail door. He is a huge and powerful man, but is handicapped by a deformity in his feet. He was born with this affliction, but with his shoes made to measure he seems to cope without too much trouble on land. However, when he's obliged to use waders, it's a different matter, and I've seen him taking some spectacular tumbles when attempting to negotiate the slobland.

He is now sitting in his 'hide' talking to Maggie. Maggie is his pet mallard duck. She's taken everywhere he takes the notion to lie in wait for wildfowl. He has her wings bound with some rabbit netting, just in case she 'takes a mad fit, and flies away'. All around her in the flash of water he has placed a number of timber decoy ducks. For some reason he cannot understand, all his guile is ineffective and the evening sky is still bereft of ducks and geese.

Maggie is siting silent and motionless in the pond of water. Suddenly the big man's patience runs out, and he roars at the duck, 'God blast you, Maggie, what's wrong with you? Are you in use or what? you son of a whore.'

The outburst had the desired effect, and Maggie began squawking and calling at the top of her voice. The squawking didn't attract any ducks, but it did reach Fly's ears, and he was now creeping quietly through the sea-weed stones like a rogue fox. Suddenly he made a rush and grabbed the duck and made off towards the hide where Pad was sitting patiently.

The big man was out of his butt in quick time and began shouting and bellowing like a man demented. 'Oh Jasus, Pad, quick. Quick, Pad. Oh Jasus, Pad, he's aten Maggie.'

The big man was wrong, and Maggie was lucky. For some reason Fly had not curled a feather on the duck and he brought her to Pad's hide and delivered her into his hand with a look of utter surprise on her face.

We prepare to leave for home. The ducks or geese are not inclined to flight. The weather is probably too mild, and they are resting out in the Shannon Estuary with nothing to disturb them. We are rowing home along the channel of the Deel Estuary. It is low water. It is now past nightfall, but is not yet completely dark. Ahead of us on the mud-bank, nine tame geese are standing, talking and muttering to each other. They are the property of a family living across the river.

When they first came into view, the big man was looking back towards the area we had just left, and was not paying any attention to his front. His companion (the chap from the village) suddenly whispered, 'Christ, look at the geese.' The effect on the big man was electric. He had a magnificent American five-shot repeater that a friend had purchased for him several years before.

At the word 'geese' he threw this gun to his shoulder, not yet having focused on the actual position of the birds. 'Where are they? Where are they?' he said.

My father turned on him. 'Take care,' he said, 'and don't touch those geese, they're tame.'

The big man had now drawn a bead on the nine white geese. Under his breath he said, 'Tame, my arse,' then he commenced firing. If he had taken his time, he probably would have inflicted much more havoc than he actually did; as it was, three geese remained lying stone dead on the mud; the remaining six ran screaming for their lives towards the shore.

The contrast the effect of the shooting had on the second man in the boat, and Pad, was unbelievable. For a moment I thought Pad would strike the big man with an oar. 'Christ Almighty,' he said, 'what did you do that to me for?'

It wasn't the shooting of the geese that worried him, but the possible consequences. There was the strong possibility that the owners, seeing their flock arriving home in a wild and agitated condition, and their numbers somewhat depleted, and also perhaps having heard the shots, might just take it into their heads to make a fast trip to the village and fetch the Law. The more Pad's anger grew, the more the second visitor became convulsed with laughter, and was even now stretched his full length on the bottom of the boat, rolling, twisting and turning with mirth.

I was despatched to collect the three massive white birds from the slob. They were indeed fine specimens.

The weekend after the killing of the geese, the big sportsman made the news. The local newspaper splashed his photograph across its front page. Dressed in his full shooting regalia, he looked an impressive sight. He was holding aloft three massive white geese. The caption read: 'Famous Limerick sportsman shoots three Canadian snow geese on Shannon Estuary. These birds are rare visitors to our shores.' Rare indeed!

Several years after this incident I had occasion to visit this man's home. After a long and very interesting discussion on wildfowling, he invited me to inspect an enclosure at the rear of his premises where he kept 'his birds'. Sure enough, he had there some very interesting specimens. Maggie, now beginning to show her age, was still to the fore; also several breeds of pheasant of a type I had not seen previously.

As we were admiring this menagerie, out from the midst of the group strolled a barnacle goose, minus a wing. My curiosity aroused, I enquired as to its origins, and was informed he had been shot two years previously and had suffered a broken wing. This was cut off at the affected area and the wound very shortly healed. The bird certainly looked in the best of health.

As was usual, I, not being able to keep my mouth shut, decided to twist the big man's tail, and remarked it was a pity he hadn't one of the tame geese he shot down the river to go with this lot. His face grew black with anger and if I hadn't stepped back fast I might have been the recipient of a fast cure for a hard cough. However, after much placating, he was prevailed upon to accept the remark as a joke, which of course it was not.

This man had been frequenting our shooting area long before I was

82

capable of holding a fowling-piece. He had a fascination for the punt and gun, and was indeed a fair exponent of the art of fowling using this equipment. It was quite in order for him to prepare and load the great gun and take to the river in pursuit of ducks and geese when he so desired, even when Pad was not in a position to accompany him.

Just such an arrangement had been agreed several years before the incident of the tame geese. It was on St Stephen's Day when the big man arrived at our house to find Pad already left for the Fowler Rock with a group of shooters. With the companion he had brought along for that day's shooting he now prepared to load the mighty puntgun for an assault on the estuary. What followed was entered in the shooting lore of the area as a very comical and amusing incident. Speaking as one that became involved in it, there didn't seem anything funny about it at the time.

If the big man had used his head, he would have realised that there was already a group of poppers banging away at the Fowler Rock, and the likelihood of getting a punt-gun shot was very remote, as most wildfowl would long since have been driven out of the area. However, if everyone did what they are supposed to do, it would indeed be a dull old world.

The big man and his companion took to the river in the punt and rowed away to the north, and in spite of the fact that they did not fire the big gun, they had a very enjoyable day, until they began their journey home.

As I've mentioned previously, the handling of a shooting punt when weighed down with equipment and, in this case, two extra heavy men, needs close attention. Proceeding homewards in pitch darkness, helped by a raging spring tide, the big man was sitting on the stern using the punting paddle; his companion was midships, rowing with the two small oars.

Both men were heavy smokers. As they were negotiating the river at its widest point, the man rowing suddenly stowed his oars and produced his cigarettes. He stood up and took three paces towards his companion on the stern. Now, the least amount of buoyancy in a shooting punt is at the stern and with the boat carrying only three inches of clear-board at this point, when the combined weight of both men was concentrated here, the stern went under water and the boat filled and sank.

I was sitting at the fire with the rest of the family waiting for Pad's return when a commotion began at the front door. The mother went to investigate and I heard her gasp, 'God almighty, what happened to you?'

The agitated voice of the big man answered, 'Oh Jasus, missus, don't ask me. Don't ask me, missus, don't ask me.' The mother retreated into the kitchen followed by the big man. He looked a sorry sight, with mud and water dripping from his face and clothes, pieces of seaweed clung to his coat.

In the light of the kitchen, the mother asked again, 'What happened to you?' The big man looked forlornly back at her. 'She fell asunder, mam,' he said, 'she fell asunder.' 'What fell asunder?' the mother asked. 'The ould boat, mam,' he said. 'She must be rotten, she fell asunder and sank like a stone. I had to swim for it, mam, Jasus, I had to swim for it.' The mother's hand went to her throat and her face paled. 'Where is the man that went with you?' she asked.

The big man was obviously suffering from severe shock. 'He's drowned, mam,' he said. 'He's drowned, they're all drowned. The ould boat was rotten, it fell asunder, mam.'

The mother looked at me. 'Quick,' she said, 'get Pad.' 'How will I get Pad?' I asked. 'Don't you know he went to the Fowler with the lads.' 'Go and look for him,' she said, 'and never mind your old gab.'

The big man was ushered into the back room, where a clothes-line reaching from wall to wall held an assortment of wearing apparel. His choice of underwear was inappropriate, and the mother was soon obliged to go to his assistance in the room where he was tied up in a knot, attempting to force his huge bulk into a little confirmation dress belonging to my sister. 'Jasus, missus,' he said, 'this little shirt must belong to Danny (this was the name he would insist in calling me).'

The mother came from the room and gave me a dirty look. 'I told you to go and look for Pad,' she said. 'I won't tell you again.' I left the house and ran to the quay. No sign of a boat. I held my breath and listened, not a sound. The night was dead calm, yet not a sound of human voice or an oar rocking in a rowlock. I ran along the strand of the Deel Estuary, stumbling and staggering, then I listened again. Faintly, in the distance I heard the sound of voices. As they grew louder I began to halloa at the top of my voice until finally an answering 'Halloa' reached me. Soon the boat pulled in where I was standing and in the midst of the group on board was a mud-and-water-soaked man I recognised as the big man's partner in the shooting punt that morning.

When the two men were standing in the stern of the punt in the act of lighting their cigarettes, we can only imagine their surprise and shock when they found their life support gone and they were left struggling in the water. In complete panic, both struck out in different directions, not having a clue where they were heading. How they survived was a miracle. Both men were prepared for any weather, with heavy winter clothing and top boots or waders. The big man had on a 'poacher's' coat. These are magnificent three-quarter-length coats (they were marketed under this name). The coat was of a heavy green material, and the inside lining was one huge pocket. The big man had stored in this pocket two hundred cartridges. Why these, combined with his heavy clothing and top boots, did not take him straight to the bottom is something I'll never know. He began swimming and crawling through the ice-cold water until he reached the shallows, and then struck off through the mudlands until he arrived at our house.

The second man, finding himself in the water, swam in the opposite direction, to the east, and away from land. He too had on the heavy winter clothing and waders, but was not handicapped by the weight of cartridges. His guardian angel was certainly at work, as he hadn't gone far when his feet touched bottom and he crawled onto a half-submerged rock, and there he remained, crying and calling, until overheard by Pad and his cronies on their way home from the Fowler Rock.

At low water next morning, the punt was recovered, lying on the mud where it had been mismanaged and drowned. The punting paddle and oars were on the shore at high-water mark. Far from being 'rotten' and 'falling asunder' as the shock-crazed visitor assumed, the boat outlived him and is still with us.

Thirteen

Overhead the classroom where Rooney rules with a fist of iron and the ashplant is the Girls' School.

In contrast to the garrulous and insulting attitude of Rooney, the girls are in the tender care of a kind-hearted lady called Miss Wall. Not being handicapped by a family of her own she has devoted all her time and energies to improving the lot of the girls under her care.

One of her pet subjects is dressmaking. To improve the girls' capability at this very necessary attribute, she has requisitioned the help of a dressmaker from the village. This dressmaker has two sons in our classroom, and after school in the afternoon they are obliged to visit the local flour mill in search of discarded and broken flour bags for their mother.

From these flour bags, the dressmaker and the teacher can produce the most amazing clothing for the girls. Underwear of all sorts, also pinafores, bed sheets, pillow covers, table cloths, and indeed all types of usables. The material these sacks were made from was called calico. It had one major drawback: it was difficult to remove the brand name. Even after dyeing, the outline of the brand could be seen. It was a strange sight on a windy day, as a group of girls were on their way to or from school, when a sudden gust of wind would send a skirt or dress awry, to see a flour-brand displayed, front or back.

On a visit to this dressmaker's house one evening after school, I was amazed to hear her inform a woman customer that she would be all ready for the winter now, and the east wind would not reach her, as she had put Victor at her arse and John Harris-Russell at her belly! It was some time later I realised these were popular brands of flour.

The dressmaker's wedding ring had been utilised to marry twenty-seven couples in the village. Why people that could not even rise to the cost of a wedding ring should even contemplate marriage is beyond understanding. One such couple produced twenty-two children.

A young woman, arriving at the dressmaker's house to borrow the ring, provoked the long-suffering woman to comment on the bleak prospects of the intended groom. 'In God's name, Annie,' she said, 'what are ye going to live on?'

Annie thought for a while and then replied, 'I'll tell you, mam, the way I look at it, sure if I haven't a thing to eat itself, I'll have something to look at.'

The dressmaker muttered under her breath. 'That's all right, Annie, if you haven't a lot of things to look at.'

As Annie was the first of her family to marry, her father decided to throw a little party. His profession was 'scallop-maker', an employment not geared towards riches. The guests were expected to fetch their own 'dream-maker', in this instance, as much porter as possible, stored in buckets.

The house consisted of one 'compartment' – meaning one room! It was built against the sheer face of a cliff, and for this reason the roof and chimney were within easy reach of the field at the rear of the house. As the night progressed, and more and more visitors crowded into the little house, carrying their buckets of dream juice, the seating accommodation became desperate. Against the wall was a heap of turnips. These were now being used as a precarious resting-place by a number of the revellers. The firing used by the household was the green tops of the hazel sticks used to make the scallops. As one might expect, these greens were terrific smoke-makers.

As the black fluid began to take its toll, the urge for devilment took holt of some of the gathering, and a group of men slipped outside, robbing a sack from near the door as they left. The door was pulled out and bolted on the outside, and the group of revellers then scrambled quickly up the cliff face, and in less time than it takes to relate, had thrown the sack over the chimney.

The result of their caper was not at once apparent to those left in the house, until someone remarked that the chimney had developed a puff-down. In minutes, fuelled by the sap-laden greens, the kitchen was thick with smoke. In the mad rush to get out, the contents of the house were put flying. The first to be scattered were the turnips. These acting like marbles under the feet of the intoxicated throng, people were upended in all directions. The scallop-maker, believing the prank had been played from inside the house, reached over the fireplace and took down the reaping hook he used to cut the hazel rods, and began making wild swipes at the dim outlines of heads and backs.

'Clear out, ye sons of whores,' he shouted, 'clear out, or I'll have yer noppers.'

The gathering in the house would be only too willing to leave, given the chance, but all attempts to open the door went for naught.

The man nearest the door was known in local jargon as Sweet-Puss. He made a sound deep in his throat as if he was sucking a luscious mouthful, then he tapped politely on the door. 'I say, you out there,' he said sweetly, 'would you open this door if you please, I say, if you please, would you open this door?' The only reply from outside was a loud guffaw of wild drunken laughter.

Things in the house were still flying about, and the scallop-maker was still cutting the air with the reaping hook. Some of the revellers had fainted from the effects of the thick choking smoke. Suddenly, Sweet-Puss was grabbed from the rear and thrown aside. A group of men gathered themselves into a battering-ram and crashed into the door, sending it flying outwards onto the pranksters outside. The resulting mad rush over the fallen door by those trapped inside left the perpetrators wishing they had given Annie's wedding party a miss.

Fourteen

Jim Brody's uncle has an artifical leg. He lost his leg in the American army when he was run over by a horse-drawn gun carrige. It's not an artificial limb in the true sense of the word, as it's merely a lump of seasoned elm. It has to be replaced fairly regularly and he has an arrangement with a handyman down the road for this purpose. When Jim's uncle has obtained a supply of porter in sufficient quantity to curb his awesome thirst, he will fix himself in his favourite sugain chair before the fire in the kitchen hearth and sleep the night away. However, while searching with his feet, artificial and otherwise, for bedclothes that are not there, his wooden leg will find its way into the greesock (embers) with the resulting consequence. The handyman down the road that provides these limbs is usually kept busy when this individual receives his American pension.

Brody was obliged (like many others), to flee the country in his youth, and was lucky to reach the 'Land of the Free' with a whole skin. In the locality at the time was a tyrant landlord. His misdeeds were legion, as he used his powers of landlord and magistrate to the full. It was the days of secret organisations, when the Irish formed themselves into bands in an effort to prevent a powerful enemy from banishing them from the face of the earth, or at least from the face of Ireland. It was the enemy's intention to turn this green and fruitful country into a vast beef-ranch to provide meat for an army bent on world domination. Jim Brody's uncle was sucked into one such organisation by an event which took place on the night of his father's funeral.

As the remains were being taken to the church, borne on the shoulders of neighbours, and followed by the people of the district, on foot and on donkeys and carts, the cortège was obliged to pass by the gate of the landlord. Fate, as she usually does, decided to take a hand in the proceedings. As the multitude was passing by the landlord's gate, the tyrant chose that exact moment to make a journey to the village for a supply of pipe tobacco. He was mounted on a magnificent colt, barely broken to the saddle. As the high-spirited animal was confronted by the throng, he took fright, and attempted to retreat back through the gateway.

The landlord was not having any of this. He would not be pushed off the road by a rabble of half-starved beggars. In his hand he carried a heavy bull whip, a lash from which was sufficient to lay a man's buttocks open to the bone. He now commenced to cut a path through the funeral cortège, using this whip like a scythe through corn. People screamed and fled in all directions; children were knocked and trampled on; legs, hands, and faces were torn open by briers and bushes as the mourners tried to get out of reach of that flailing whip. Jim Brody's uncle felt the lash that laid his thigh open and allowed the blood to run freely onto the roadway.

Amongst the throng was Pad (he was of the same age group as Brody). When the tyrant had finally worked his way through the crowd, leaving behind a trail of pain and misery, and carried on unconcerned towards the village, Pad stood on the ditch at the side of the road gazing after the proud unassailable figure. The funeral picked itself up and carried on towards the Chapel, but Pad still remained standing on the ditch, gazing along the road where the horseman could no longer be seen.

The day the coffin was put in the earth, and the neighbours were returning to their homes, Pad waylaid Brody who was hobbling along the roadway leading to his house, his leg still smarting from the lash.

Pad did not beat about the bush. 'What do you intend doing about that shyster?' he asked.

Brody looked at him vacantly. 'What can we do?' he said. 'Isn't he the law, can't he do what he likes?'

'I'll tell you what can be done,' Pad told him. 'Whether he's the law or not, we'll shoot him.'

Brody's face paled. 'Do you realise what you are saying?' he asked. 'How in the name of God can we do that?'

Pad looked at him for a moment. 'It's easy,' he said. 'You use a thing called a gun.'

The seeds having been sown, the plan soon began to take shape. The secret organisation of the area was brought into the plan and offered to help in any way it could. All the landlord's habits were mapped out. Most of this information was acquired from workers on the estate. It was ascertained that he visited the village on two nights of the week, Tuesdays and Fridays, on horseback. On these occasions, he carried with him a little carbide lamp, and on his way home this lamp was slung from a strap round his shoulder. It was decided that this lamp would be the source of his identification and destruction. On the night chosen to shoot him, word would be passed through the locality that the residents should remain in their houses lest a mistake be made. But the best-laid plans are open to human error; one cannot think of everything.

On a small farm near the estate of the landlord was in employment a little wizened man who made a profession of pinching anything saleable from his employer, and carrying it to the village to sell for porter. On the night chosen to do the deed, he had 'knocked off' a sack of oats. To transport the oats to the village he had 'borrowed' the farmer's donkey. This little man, as well as having an awesome thirst for porter, was also terrified of the dark, and as fate would have it, had also in his possession a carbide lamp identical to that of the landlord. He was not privy to the deadly plan intended to remove his tyrant neighbour from the face of the planet once and for all.

At the appointed time, Pad and Brody took their place behind a hedge which grew on a high bank near the roadway leading from the village to the landlord's estate. They had a clear view of the road for some distance in both directions. It was a bitterly cold night, making a black frost. The guns to be used were two ordinary muzzle-loading fowling pieces, not the most effective for the job in hand, but the best available. They had cleaned and loaded these weapons at Brody's house earlier in the evening, the routine of which I have already covered. They had taken up positions fifty yards apart, with Brody at the village end of the ambuscade. If the landlord should escape his fire, the second gun would finish him off.

They stood and waited in the bitter cold, shivering in their clothes, as much from the thought of the intended deed as the actual cold. The time passed slowly, and then suddenly round the distant bend of the road a faint yellow glow appeared.

The eyes of the watching pair stared at it as if hypnotised. Relentlessly the bobbing light drew nearer, and the faint double 'click-click' of muzzle-locks was heard on the frosty night air. As the light came slowly into Brody's range, both gunmen gave an inaudible gasp – rounding the bend in the distance, bobbing slowly along, came a second light. There was nothing in the prepared plan to cope with this situation. Brody left his perch and trotted along the hedge to where Pad was waiting.

Through chattering teeth he whispered, 'What will we do, Pad? There's two of the bastards.'

The horseman in front was now passing underneath them, the glow from the little carbide lamp casting an eerie shadow around man and horse. He was now beginning to draw away, and would soon be out of range. The second light drew steadily closer. Which was the landlord? – that was the problem now facing the two watching men.

The queston was solved by the raucous roar of a stallion ass that came from the area of the second light. That settled it, it was obvious that the horseman that had passed, and was now drawing away into the night, was the landlord. As if by an unheard command, both men placed their fowling-pieces to their shoulders, took what aim they could at the now distant and dim figure on horseback and pulled the triggers of their muzzle-loaders.

The resulting crash of sound was carried far and wide on the still frosty air, it echoed through the houses and cabins of the area. What did it entail? Were the people at last rid of the tyrant?

The two gunmen did not investigate the condition of their victim, one thing they were agreed on, the man they fired on had toppled from his horse and did not rise again, while the pounding hoofbeats of the frightened animal could be heard fading into the distance.

They retreated across country towards home. The news reached them at mid-day; the landlord had survived the attack. The little man on the stallion ass had saved his life. He found him lying on the roadside, his head in a pool of blood. With difficulty he placed him on the back of the donkey, and returned to the village, where the local doctor plucked eighteen grains of shot from his neck and head. The pause by the gunmen, trying to ascertain which of the lamp-carriers was their target, had saved his life, by placing him *just* outside the killing range of their guns.

With the landlord's recovery came also a change in his attitude. No longer was he the scourge of his tenants, or indeed the unfortunates that came before his bench in the course of his magistrate's duties. He looked on his escape as Divine Intervention, and turned from being a demon into a sociable and out-going character.

Not so the police. After the attack, they began the greatest comb-out of the countryside ever seen in the area. Hedges, ditches, fields and woodlands were minutely searched for anything that might give a clue to the identities of the assailants. Next came the houses. One by one they were gone over.

As the search continued, a strange story began to spread through the

92

countryside behind the search parties. Almost all the police involved seemed to have an uncanny interest in reading; at least, in any house where books were found, the contents of these had been thoroughly examined.

Finally, on the Saturday morning following the attack, the searchers arrived at the Brody homestead. The police were polite but thorough. The interest in books found in the house was at once apparent. Suddenly, one of the searchers gasped, and called the sergeant in charge to examine a tattered volume, its title, *The Tenants' Rights of Tipperary*. The sergeant pulled a piece of smoke-blackened paper from his pocket and smoothed it on the kitchen table; he placed the well-read volume beside it and then carefully placing the blackened paper against a torn page, he grunted with satisfaction – the two pieces matched exactly.

On the morning following the attempted killing, the police carefully examined the area in the vicinity of the shooting. Two clues immediately presented themselves. The first was the clear boot-marks of one of the assailants which had obviously been well-studded with shamrock-shaped nails. The second was a piece of smoke-blackened paper stuck in a whitethorn bush. It was recognised by its appearance, and smell, as having been used to hold a charge of shot in place in a muzzle-loading gun. After careful examination of this clue, the police were convinced that the gunman or gunmen had made a dastardly blunder. If the book that this torn piece of paper was taken from could be located, then, surely, the evidence of guilt would be irrefutable.

The police sergeant looked round Brody's kitchen with a look of utter satisfaction on his porter-reddened face; he could afford to be smug. He ran his eyes over the feet of the assembled Brody family. The younger members were bare-footed, these he ignored. His eyes focused on a strapping young man near the door, he stooped and grabbed his trouser leg, and as if he was addressing a horse about to be shod, he barked, 'Give it up,' pulling the lad's leg off the ground and carefully examining the sole of the boot. After a moment he released it and, with a grunt of barely concealed delight, exclaimed, 'Arrest him.'

Brody's hands were pulled roughly behind him and the iron manacles snapped over his wrists, to the utter consternation of his mother, who fell on her knees and grabbed the sergeant by the legs and implored him to leave her son be, as she had just recently lost her husband and all this trouble was too much for her.

The policeman shook her free of his trouser leg and shouted, 'You should have thought of that before you allowed him to get mixed up with the Fenian bastards. You have the makings of a right murderer here, missus,'

To be fair, it must be said the police sergeant was a humane man. Brody was taken with the minimum of force and lodged in the 'black hole' which was the local title for the police-barracks 'lock-up' or 'holding-room'. No chances were being taken however, and he was secured by his manacles to a steel ring which was firmly planted in the cell wall.

The police sergeant and his men were over the moon with delight at the capture, and adjourned to their favourite pub to celebrate. It must be admitted it was good police work, to deduce from the piece of blackened paper found in the whitethorn hedge that it had been used in the gun that had almost put paid to the landlord, and then follow up this lead to the house of the assailant.

As the porter flowed freely in the pub, they decided to show a little hospitality, and engaged a local woman to prepare a meal and take it to the prisoner at the barrack. The woman arrived to find the building almost deserted, with just one young policeman on duty in the day room.

She addressed herself to the young man without more ado: 'The sergeant sent me up with grub for the fellow in the hole.'

The policeman took a bunch of keys from the drawer in the blue coloured table before him. 'Follow me,' he told her, and led her along a stone-flagged passage to a stout wooden door at the end. He pushed a large key into the lock and turned it.

The door swung open to reveal Brody sitting on three planks of wood that rested on two iron frames sticking from the wall. His hands were secured to the metal ring behind his back, and the effect of this was immediately obvious. His trousers were soaked with urine. The cell did have a hole in the corner of the floor, which gave it its name. This led into an open sewer, running across the narrow field between the barracks and the Deel river, but it was of little use to the prisoner in his present predicament. The woman, seeing the condition of the prisoner, rounded on the young policeman, 'You dirty bocock,' she shouted, 'what way is that to treat any man, whatever he's supposed to have done? Get them irons off that poor man and let him have his tae.'

The young policeman had been reared in a house where his mother's word was law, he had often felt the sting of her work-hardened hands across his face. Being a dutiful son he had accepted her orders and instructions without question and he now fell back into the mould of his youthful conditioning. Without a murmur he turned and left the cell;

the harsh-voiced woman had stripped away his police training and left him once again a brow-beaten youth in his mother's kitchen. He went to the day room and collected the keys to the handcuffs.

The woman in the cell whispered rapidly to Brody, 'The Shadogue is here on his own, now is your time if you're ever going to get away.'

With his hands free, and the blood again flowing to his numbed arms and fingers, Brody began to munch the food left by the woman of the village. Her words were still knocking around inside his head, 'now is your chance to get away'.

The policeman had relocked the cell door after the woman left, and returned to the day room to await his colleagues' return. Brody looked round his dimly-lit cell, the only light came from a small barred window high on the wall, it was hardly large enough to allow a cat to escape, never mind a large man. If there was any going out of this prison, it was through the doorway. He examined the door carefully, it was constructed of stout oak planking, and was in fact almost indestructible. It was six and a half feet high, and dead in its centre was an opening something akin to a modern-day letter-box, only this one did not have a weather flap. This opening was the spyhole.

Brody examined it carefully, he removed a plank from the cell 'bed' and placed it against the opening, he found it fitted easily.

He thought fast. The woman of the village was correct; if he was ever to escape it must be now, before the remainder of the 'Shadogues' returned from the pub, and the transport was arranged for his removal to the prison in the city, where, he was well aware, would commence the process of obtaining from him the names of his accomplices. He did not fool himself into thinking that they would be long in prising this information loose.

He began to bang on the door with his fist, and also used his steel-shod boots to attract the attention of the constable.

The policeman approached along the passageway. 'What's up with you?' he shouted. Brody replied, 'This hole is full of rats, give me some kind of light to frighten them.'

The lawman stooped and peeped through the spyhole, he could see the dim outline of the prisoner sitting on his bunk. He pushed the key into the lock and turned it. Then he made a fatal error. He looked again through the spyhole. Brody had already the plank from the bunk resting just below the slot in the door; with all his senses on full alert, he guessed rather than saw the policeman's face return for a second look. At that precise moment, he shot the plank through the peep-hole. The force of the blow from this desperate man sent the lawman flying backwards, and he crashed into the sidewall of the passage. He fell to the ground unconscious, blood flowing from his forehead.

Brody was out of his cell and sprinting through the passage without a second glance at his victim.

He had other things to worry him. From the lane leading from the village to the barrack could be heard the loud porter talk of the returning policemen. Escape through the front of the building was out of the question. He ran through the back doorway and entered the barrack yard. Here he was confronted by a twelve-foot wall. He didn't hesitate, he ran with all his strength, and using the momentum of speed, scrambled up its face and gained a grip at the top. Broken bottles had been set in mortar all along this wall, and these reefed the hands of the fleeing man.

He bounded onto the field and raced towards the river. The Deel was in flood, but Brody did not hesitate, he plunged in, and being a powerful swimmer, moments later he flashed under the village bridge, his head barely showing above the earth-brown floodwater.

At the time this event took place, a businessman in the village was carrying on a lively trade, importing coal in small coaster vessels from Britain and the continent of Europe, and exporting on the same vessels what was called at the time, 'pressed hay', or as we call it now 'baled hay'. As Brody came tearing along the river, one of these vessels was being made ready for sea at the quayside of Gurt. It was bound for France.

The water-logged man was pulled aboard, and with the hue and cry already spreading through the countryside, the ship's pilot made the situation known to the captain. When the vessel left that evening on its journey to France, Brody was well stowed away amongst the bales of hay. From France, he made his way to America's free shore.

When Brody had been arrested, he was wearing a type of bawneen jumper, handmade for him by his mother. As luck would have it – or if you like, ill luck – a cowman employed by a dairy in the village also had one of this type of garment. As the drink-crazed policemen fanned out from the barrack, mad with rage at the escape of their prized prisoner and the attack on their colleague, our cowman was making his way through high ground north of the village to collect his employer's cows for evening milking. Suddenly, the ground around him was cleaved with bullets. The cowman carried on unconcerned, not realising the danger of his predicament. A bullet striking off the limestone wall a short distance to his right, and ricocheting past his nose like an angry wasp, made him take stock of his situation in a hurry, and he dived headlong into a clump of briers, from where he was pulled some time later by a group of very disappointed policemen.

There is no doubt that the amount of drink consumed by the policemen affected their aim, thereby saving the life of the cowman. There is also no doubt that the confusion caused by this incident helped Brody in no small way to reach the coaster unobserved, and thereby make his escape.

Fifteen

The Sodality was organised in the local church to give a new slant of religious fervour to a people already suffering from a surfeit of religion. However, the Irish, never content to do anything in moderation, took to this method of public piety with their usual enthusiasm. Worshippers were formed into platoons, with their own officers and NCOs.

The women of the parish took to this form of public display with much more gusto than their menfolk; after all, it was one more opportunity to display their finery, under the guise of piety. The Sodality members, both men and women, wore a red ribbon round their shoulders. At the end of this ribbon was the Sodality medal. The officers in charge of each group were responsible for ensuring the attendance of their members at the Sodality Mass and Communion. These officers were readily recognisable by a ribbon much larger than those of the mere members. The attached medal was proportionately of suitable dimensions.

Over all these Sodality members was the 'Supreme Officer Commanding'. On the women's side, this was the wife of a substantial farmer some distance from the village. She arrived at church each Sunday morning, dressed in a manner pertinent to her lofty position. She wore a beautiful three-quarter-length fox-fur coat, and on her head rested a little green hat made from the exotic feathers of some foreign bird. Her ribbon was made from the finest material. She did indeed look the copy-book image of what a proper OC should be.

As the Sodality was moving from strength to strength, with its numbers growing all the time, as those holding back were being forced to join, lest public odium brand themselves and their families, or even – horror of horrors – have their names shouted from the altar, a strange plague began to strike down the cattle at the western end of the parish.

At the time, veterinarians were a rare species, if not nonexistent. Numerous suggestions were put forward by so-called 'experts'. A poisonous weed, 'black quarter', bad water, and so on. But still the animals died, to such a degree that many farmers in the area were reduced almost to beggary. Then one fine morning, a farmer with a bit more sense than the rest took careful stock of one of his dead cows. He noticed a slight trace of blood from the vaginal passage. He investigated further, and a strange suspicion began to take shape in his mind. His wife, having come from the house to console him, had her own ideas. She had been reared on the Limerick–Kerry border where pishoguery was rife at the time, and she now attempted to convince her husband of the likelihood of this explanation.

Her husband would not buy it. 'I think, Mary,' he said, 'there's more than pishoguery going on here.'

He went to the kitchen and fetched the butchering knife used to cut up the bacon, and with a few fast cuts laid open the stomach of the dead animal. Two clues as to the cause of death presented themselves. The abdominal cavity was full of blood, and on closer examination it was found the cow's womb was ruptured, obviously having been run through with a sharp instrument. The revelation struck the farmer like a hammer blow, and then a cold anger gripped his heart. This was no accident, and yet, if what his brain was now telling him was true, what type of demon was perpetrating these deeds?

It was obvious, or at least almost obvious, that he had stumbled on the cause of the affliction that had decimated the cattle of the surrounding farmers. He spent the remainder of the day visiting his neighbours and relating his suspicions. Some were frankly incredulous. What was he suggesting? That some kind of maniac was at large in the area, busily destroying the livelihood of the farmers?

But this farmer was a cut above his neighbours when cold logic was required. He began going back over certain incidents that had taken place. All the cattle, or nearly all, had had the tell-tale sign of blood from one or another of the back passages; most of the cattle that had died were milk-cows; all of these cows had been stalled in their byres at the time; and last, but perhaps the strangest phenomenon of all, all the cattle died on Sundays, mostly during the time of Second Mass in the village, when all these farms were deserted.

His neighbours began to sit up and take notice. Had this man hit on the answer? Was this the explanation?

Then they too became crazy with rage. They would go out into the countryside and find this 'cow-killer' whoever he was, and give him the same as he had given to their unfortunate animals. One farmer rammed the poker into the greesock on the hearth until it glowed blood-red, to show what he would do to the killer that had left him almost penniless. But again the cold logic of the neighbour came into play.

'Where would we start?' he wanted to know. 'How would we go about finding this demon? No, gentlemen, this job requires a professional. There is nothing to be gained in forming ourselves into a mob and going about the countryside, not knowing who or what we are looking for. As it was I that came up with this idea in the first place, I would ask ye to let me run with it for a while longer. I will make a trip to the village to see a friend of mine in the police. I don't believe one should go to bed with the same police, but they can be very useful at times like these. They have methods of getting information that we never even heard of.'

The farmer arrived at the flat of his policeman friend at nine o'clock that night. The man himself answered his knock, and showed him into a little room at the back. The policeman had been in the process of polishing his boots, and was in his stockinged feet. He had two school-going daughters, and these were now sitting at a little table engaged in what appeared their home exercise. Their father spoke gently: 'Leave us alone for a while, girls, I want to have a chat with this man.' His daughters smiled at the visitor and left the room.

The policeman had come to the village ten years before, with his wife and daughters. He came from the midlands. It was at that station he had met his future wife, and from the first, he was completely captivated by her. She was small and cuddly and hot as fire, and the sexual pleasure she had given him during their early years of marriage had surpassed even his wildest dreams.

He was a convert to her faith, but to him it did not entail the slightest sacrifice to abandon his Protestant faith for her Roman Catholic beliefs. For the past two years, however, his life had become a Hell on earth. That was the length of time his wife was a member of the Sodality. The change at first was so gradual he hardly noticed, and then, as the weeks passed, she became more and more withdrawn. He liked his porter, this policeman; not to excess, just a few pints at night, and usually in the company of the farmer now sitting across the fire from him. He had come home one night to find the house in darkness and the fire dead. This was unusual in the extreme, but worse was to follow.

When he went to the bedroom and got in beside his wife, and

attempted to put his arms around her, she drew away as if he were a leper.

'Keep away from me,' she almost shouted. 'You're stinking with sour porter, and I'm not going to stand for any more of this. Coming in at all hours of the night and thinking you'll behave like an animal with me. If ye do that in your religion, you needn't think you'll get away with it with me. Father Hartigan was right, no woman should allow a man get up on top of her and his belly full of porter and do those awful things.'

The policeman couldn't believe his ears. At first he thought she was joking, but a closer look at her drawn features and rigid limbs left him in no doubt as to her attitude. Could this be his lovable wife that until quite recently had been such a joy to live with?

He looked at her closely. 'Joan,' he said, 'remember me, I'm your husband, you know, the man that loves you.' She cut him short.

'Love me?' she spat at him through clenched teeth. 'You don't know the meaning of the word, all you want is what all drunken bums want, a cheap thrill when they're hunted home from the pubs, oh indeed, Father Hartigan was right.'

'For God's sake, Joan,' he began, but she cut across him again.

'Don't you talk about God, it's only now my eyes are opened. Down in the pubs every night with your pals, whore-houses would be a better name for them, but the Sodality will put a stop to yer gallop, Father Hartigan will see that those houses of sin will get what's coming to them.'

She sprang onto the floor and moved towards the room door. He tried again to put his arm round her. 'Keep away,' she said, 'or the whole street will hear me.' With that parting shot she ran from the room and entered the bedroom of her daughters who were sitting up in bed, holding tightly to each other, unable to understand this sudden upheaval in their family's fortunes.

The policeman remained standing staring at the closed door. What in God's name had happened to turn his easy-going peaceful way of life upside down? What was that name she kept repeating? 'Father Hartigan', 'the Sodality' – was that it? Was that what had soured his wife and turned her into a bitching middle-aged woman? Even her appearance was different. He was seeing again the bitter puckering of her mouth as she spat out her accusations at him, the hunching of her shoulders, the gathering of her arms across her breasts, as if to protect those vessels of femininity from the eyes of a sex-crazed maniac.

He dropped into a chair beside the bed and held his head in his hands.

He'd had a feeling for some time that something like this was in the offing, but the accusations! As if he would ever think of his wife with anything but the greatest esteem. He'd placed her far and above the failings of ordinary mortals, and now this. Who put such notions into her head? Why should religious attitudes always assume that anything giving pleasure, sex, drink, smoking, or indeed any pleasurable activity, must necessarily be sinful?

He removed his boots and lay down on the bed, but sleep evaded him. He had worked hard at his marriage, building it up with the bricks of kindness and understanding, until he believed he had reached a pinnacle where it was unassailable, and now this! How could the years of closeness, friendship, secrets shared, the begetting of two beautiful daughters and all that entailed, suddenly be smashed to rubble at his feet? The policeman did not fool himself, he was convinced that his marriage had received a body blow from which it would never recover. After a long time, he fell into a troubled sleep.

As the days passed, the policeman began to see that his hopes of things reverting to their previous peaceful ways were wishful thinking. There was no going back. Even when he remained home from the pub, it was looked on by his wife as a ruse to get her back into his bed and take up where they had left off. The home scene now began to show on the face of the policeman. From being a likable jolly man, he became dour and sour. During his periods of duty in the village, when he observed the crowds on their way to the Chapel, a cold anger gripped his heart at what he considered was their hypocritical piety.

As the farmer sat across the fire from his friend, he could see the ravages of the past two years on his face, but yet he could sense that the policeman was glad to see him. It was as if he might help to remove, if only for a short while, the death-like feeling that had settled over his household since that terrible night in the bedroom.

'Will you drink a mouthful of whiskey, Mick?' he asked, and then, forgetting for a moment his misery, he went on, 'On second thought, you better have a small one, that mouth of yours would hold a half gallon.'

Both men laughed long and loud, and then, taking a swig from his whiskey, the farmer looked closely at the policeman. 'I suppose you've heard what's been happening to the cows back west?' he asked.

'I heard, Mick,' he said. 'A bad business. Did ye get any clue as to what was causing it?'

The farmer played with his whiskey glass as if wondering where to begin with his strange tale, and then, being the hard-headed type he was, decided to relate the story start to finish as he'd put it together in his head, and so he began.

When he was finished, the lawman remained silent for some time, watching his visitor from under bushy brows, then he spoke. 'Mick,' he said, 'are you gone clear off your head or what? Are you seriously trying to tell me that there is someone going around your area killing off the cows? And what proof have you? You examined one animal, perhaps the other cattle died from some natural cause?'

The farmer finished off his whiskey and held out his glass to the policeman. 'Throw another drop in that,' he said, and then, settling back in his chair, remarked, 'How do you account for the Sunday morning business? Surely you're not suggesting this is sheer coincidence?'

The lawman leaned forward in his chair. 'Mick,' he asked, 'what type of neighbours are back there? Surely you must see that to me, looking in from the outside, your theory is a bit hard to swallow? Have you any knowledge of anyone acting suspiciously? If what you're saying is true, we're dealing here with someone that is quite mad.'

The farmer looked across the fire at his friend. 'I thought of that,' he said. 'But it could be something else. Maybe we're dealing with someone that is quite bad!'

They looked at each other for some time, then the policeman went to a cubbyhole and rummaged through the bric-a-brac until he found a notebook, then returned to the fireside. 'Start again, Mick,' he said. 'And slowly this time.'

By the time the full story was written between the pages of the policeman's notebook, the bottle of whiskey had received a bad fright, and the two friends decided to adjourn to their favourite pub to cool their tonsils.

For many days, the lawman made no move to visit the area of the parish where the cows had been so mysteriously meeting their end. He was a slow plodding type, and rarely moved until he knew exactly where he was going. Again and again he went over the notes he had taken down at his fireside. The farmer had been very thorough, and now, as the policeman's trained mind began to digest the story, a strange suspicion began to dawn on him.

Reading the list of names of farmers whose cattle had been destroyed, he began to place in his mind's eye the location of each house, and where it was situated in relation to that of its neighbour. As he went over the imaginary map in his mind, one house began to appear out of focus, and for some time, the policeman could not understand why, and then it struck him. This farmer, although living in the heart of the epidemic, had not lost a single animal!

The policeman now began to focus all his attention on this farm. What did he know about this man? The village gossip had him as a hard-working prosperous farmer with only one cloud on his horizon, he had failed to make his attractive wife pregnant, after eight years of marriage. She had in turn put some of her undoubted energies and abilities into good works for the parish, and was in fact the officer in charge of the Women's Sodality! The thought brought back the cold feeling to the heart of the policeman. This woman would know his wife, perhaps could have had some hand in the tragedy that had overtaken his way of life.

Towards nightfall, the policeman was to be seen riding his bicycle in his slow deliberate fashion, along the boreen leading to the house of the childless farmer. It was his first visit there, and he noticed at once the air of prosperity that prevailed the homestead.

In answer to his knock, the farmer's wife came from the interior of the house, and looked with some surprise at the unexpected figure of a uniformed policeman. 'Yes?' she inquired. The policeman missed nothing. He had many years experience of observing people under varying circumstances. He took in her nice trim figure. Why didn't she have children? She had the build and lively appearance of a woman that would have a houseful and yet she was barren.

'God save you, mam, is himself around at all?'

She seemed to be on edge. 'He's just finishing the milking beyond in the shed. Will I go and get him for you?

'Not at all, mam,' he replied. 'I'll ramble over and have a chat with him in a minute.'

'Is there anything wrong, officer?' she asked. He couldn't be sure, but he thought he sensed a touch of anxiety in her voice.

'I'm checking up on all this trouble ye're having with cows dying and no explanation as to what's causing it. But I believe ye were lucky, mam, and have escaped so far?'

She looked him straight in the face. 'It mightn't be just luck, officer, I have great faith in prayer.'

The policeman looked at her strangely. 'It's a pity your neighbours didn't pray a bit harder, so,' he said. 'Or else they're going the wrong way about it.'

He noticed a slight flush on her cheeks, and her eyes danced as if with some strange excitement. The policeman didn't know why, but in this woman's company he had the cold feeling you get when you put on a damp shirt. Perhaps he was prejudiced, but he had the eerie feeling of being close to something evil. The policeman shivered in spite of himself and moved away from the doorway. 'I'll go down and have a chat with himself,' he said, and walked away towards the farmyard. The strange cold feeling still had him in its grip, it was as if he had been asleep since his youth, and now suddenly awakened to find himself an old man. He shivered again.

In the cowhouse, the farmer was putting the finishing touches to his nightly ritual. Milk-cans had to be covered, buckets washed, and all the necessary tasks that were part and parcel of a dairy farm completed. The sight of the policeman at the entrance to the shed made the farmer straighten up with a start. 'My God, what's up?' he asked.

'God save you,' the policeman greeted him, and moved up through the shed towards the farmer, being careful where he put his feet.

The two men looked at each other for a moment, then, 'There's nothing to worry about,' the policeman said. 'As I was telling your wife, I'm just checking around, looking for some lead regarding this problem with the cows.'

The farmer removed his cap and scratched his pole. 'Well, well,' he said, 'so Mick went to see you after all. He was here with me a few days ago, but to tell you the truth, I didn't put much faith in his idea.'

The policeman looked round the well-kept byre, at the sleek well-fed animals munching contentedly, then up at the overhead loft, packed with sweet-smelling hay. 'I wouldn't dismiss it as quickly as that,' he answered. 'At least, whatever it is, it seems to have by-passed you completely.'

The farmer's face flushed scarlet with anger. 'What are you suggesting?' he said. 'That I'd raise a finger against my neighbours or their cattle? You'd better be careful, sir, of your statements.'

The policeman took this outburst quite calmly. 'I didn't suggest anything,' he said. 'I was merely congratulating you in your good fortune.'

At the back door of the dwelling-house where she was listening intently, the sound of her husband's raised voice reached the barren woman, and she spoke in a whisper into the night air. 'Of course,' she said, 'I made a mistake, how could I be so stupid?'

As the policeman cycled back to the village, his mind was in turmoil.

Had he made a mistake? Was the strange feeling he got in the company of that woman merely a figment of his imagination? But the conditioned brain of the true policeman told him he was very close to something, even though he knew not what. Well, he had stirred up the muddy waters, and now he'd have to wait and see what came to the surface.

Shortly after darkness on Saturday night, he was moving in his slow gait through the western fields of the parish, towards the homestead of the prosperous farmer. He had laid his plans carefully. He would enter the farmyard during the hours of darkness and conceal himself in the hayloft. There he would wait out the hours of darkness. He approached the farmyard carefully. He checked for wind direction. Being a countryman bred, he knew the value of this, having no wish to draw the attention of the farm dogs to his presence.

He entered the yard from the north, and stooping behind a horse's cart, he listened. The only sound to reach his ears was the wind whispering through the branches of the apple trees on his left. He slipped across the yard and entered the cowhouse. Those blessed creatures were still contentedly munching, oblivious to the hare-brained actions of humans in their lunatic moves to destroy each other. A ladder was nailed to the end wall of the shed, and this reached the loft through an open trapdoor. When the policeman reached the loft, he moved carefully. He was in total darkness, and had no wish to plunge headlong onto the backs of the animals below. He worked his way to the end wall of the loft and settled down into the hay.

As the excitement of the previous hours began to wane, he took stock of his position. He went back over the happenings of the past week, since his farmer friend first called to his flat. What had lead him to this spot? Was it just the mere intuition of a good policeman? Or was it indeed something else entirely? Was the cold hatred he felt towards the woman of this house merely a personal grudge, because of the fact she was OC of the Women's Sodality, and in his tortured mind, had he made her responsible for the change in his woman, a woman that was once so wonderful?

The night passes slowly. He listens to the strange sounds around him. Some creature of the night scurries across his boots and he cries out and kicks at it, and then listens intently. Perhaps his cry has been heard in the house. All is quiet. He begins to doze.

The cold awakens him. What time is it? The hands of his pocket watch say twelve thirty, it must be stopped, it seems he's been here a week, but the little watch is ticking strongly. What wouldn't he give for a smoke of his pipe! My God, don't people sleep an awful lot, you never realise it until you're obliged to stay awake all night. He pulls more hay around him and soon begins to doze again. He awoke with a start. He sensed rather than saw it was daylight, something had awakened him. He listens; in an adjoining shed he hears the grunting and scuffling of a sow pig waiting to be fed. A look at his watch, six thirty, things will start happening soon.

Shortly after, a door opens and closes and he hears footsteps coming towards the byre. The farmer enters, and soon the policeman hears the high-pitched sound of milk jets striking the bottom of a galvanised bucket. He hears the farmer moving from cow to cow, humming a soft tune, only to be interrupted now and then by a bout of profanity, as a cow's tail, covered with dung, strikes the farmer across the face, for what he believed was the sheer Hell of it.

The policeman hears more footsteps, he peeps through the hay. She is standing at the cow-house door, dressed in her fox-fur coat and little green hat. 'I'm off to Mass,' she says. 'Your breakfast is on the range. I'll be home before you leave for Second Mass.'

The farmer grunts. 'Right,' he says. 'Don't forget to bring the paper.'

The farmer finishes his chores and leaves the shed. The policeman has become cramped and tense in his bed of hay; it is possible he may have to stay here all day. Still he sits and waits, with strange thoughts chasing each other through his mind. Then, towards the house he hears the sound of voices – hah, she's back! Shortly after the farmer is heard leaving for the village. A strange feeling of anticipation creeps over the policeman, it was as if all this had happened before, in another time and another life. He could almost have foretold what was now about to take place.

The barren woman entered the cow-house. She was not to be recognised as the housewife that had left some time previously for the Chapel. She was dressed in rough black clothing, and there was a strange wild look about her. Her hair, that was usually so well-groomed, was now sticking out from her head, and in her right hand, she carried a three-foot iron spike.

She moved slowly along the line of stalled cows, muttering to herself, and then, before the horrified gaze of the watching policeman, she grabbed the tail of one of those bountiful creatures, and pulling it aside, she rammed the iron spike into the vaginal passage! Again and again she rammed it backwards and forwards, and then twisted it savagely round and round. The only sound from the mortally-wounded animal was a low moan, as it began to twist and turn in its death agony.

The killer stepped back, drawing the blood-stained iron from the cow's vagina, there was a look of utter savagery about her, her teeth were bared in a wolfish snarl, and her eyes were almost popping from her head. She moved to the next cow and grabbed its tail. She had the iron raised, ready to strike again, when the policeman dropped from the loft and grabbed her by the throat. A lash of his fist sent that awful implement flying from her hand, and she found herself jammed against the wall, the sound of her rasping breath mingling with the sounds of the dying animal on the floor.

The lawman came to his senses just in time, but he was still white with shock and rage. 'You miserable bitch,' he kept shouting, 'you miserable bitch.' Finally the shaking in his limbs grew less, and he said in a trembling voice, 'Get ready, you're coming with me.'

She was leaning against the wall gasping for breath, and as the sound of his voice reached her, it seemed to arouse her as if from a deep trance. 'Oh God, no,' she wailed, 'Oh God, no. I'll do anything at all, anything you ask, anything at all, only don't do this to me, if you do I'm finished, I'm finished.'

'You're wasting your breath,' he said, 'you're not fit to be at large, you horrible creature.'

'Oh please, don't do it,' she said. 'Give me a chance, you don't know what I've put up with around here. All that mob, laughing at me going the road, and they peeping from behind their curtains. "Look at her, with her hat and three hairs. She can't have a child, you know, the womb is twisted in her, and why wouldn't it, since the day her father caught her in the barn with the big sheepdog up on top of her. He kicked the belly out of her you know."'

The policeman was staggered. Does anyone ever know what dark tunnels run through the minds of people that can put on a face of piety and normality to the outside world?

He took her by the arm and led her out of the cowhouse and towards the dwelling house.

'What am I going to tell my husband?' she wailed. 'He'll be disgraced. Look,' she said, 'come in a minute till I show you something.'

They entered the dwelling-house and she went to a richly-furnished room off the kitchen. The policeman stayed in close attendance. She removed what looked like a vanity case from a sideboard and from this she took out a type of jewel box and emptied its contents onto the table. The policeman stood in amazement as his eyes took in the little heap of golden coins lying there.

'Take them,' she said, 'they're mine, my father gave them to me when I got married. I suppose he thought it would make up for what he did to me when I was just a young girl. Take them, and let me go, for God's sake, there's seventy-eight gold sovereigns there.'

The policeman walked to the room window and looked out, he was trembling again, then in a quiet voice he said over his shoulder, 'Put away your money, mam, you're coming with me.'

Three days later, she was charged at a special court in the village. The parish priest and curate went to give evidence of her good character. Some women wept openly in the overflowing courtroom, in sympathy with that vulnerable-looking figure sitting in the dock. Others ground their teeth and nudged each other. 'Look at the sit of her, the shameless bitch, she should be burned alive!'

The sentence was two years' imprisonment.

As the policeman left the courtroom, not a hand was raised in salute, not a voice congratulated him. In later years he was vilified, not least by those farmers whose cows had been decimated. It was as if he was the culprit, and not the avenger.

As I sat on a seaweed stone in his company at the Back Butts, waiting to shoot wild geese, and Pad was getting the boat ready for our journey home, the policeman remarked to my father, 'Pad, wasn't I the fool that didn't take the seventy-eight gold sovereigns?'

Pad laid down the oar he was holding, and taking his pipe from his mouth, remarked, 'John, experience teaches, but it's a dear school. . .'

Sixteen

'Be careful, sinner, lest your words bring damnation down upon your head. Your scarlet soul is well known to the Lord. There is no leaf to cover you, no branch to shelter you from the wrath of the Lord.'

I'm standing on a wynd of hay, listening to the 'Saint' rebuking the Clareman for his lack of piety. Of course he is fighting a losing battle; as I've said, the Clareman was a thundering 'Geocock'. He is not perturbed by Tom the Saint's threats. 'Don't mind your ould gob,' he says. 'Will you answer me, for Jasus sake, are you a Priest or a Bishop?'

Tom looks him straight in the eye, with what he considered was a withering stare. 'My friend, I'm a Priest, a Bishop and a Prophet.'

'Are you higher than the Pope so?' asks the Clareman.

'The Pope takes his orders from me,' Tom tells him, 'and when I come into my inheritance, I'll build my palace back near the Chapel, but of course I must also build a nice house for my brother Jim!'

The Clareman gives me a side look. 'I think,' he says, 'you're little Antichrist!'

'Silence,' roars the Saint. 'You foul-mouthed heathen, lest your tongue be the means of your damnation.'

The Clareman again ignores this rebuke. 'Tell me, Tom,' he says, 'do you ever get a notion for a bit of it at all?'

The Saint looks at him, puzzled. 'A bit of what?' he asks.

'Don't act so innocent,' the Clareman replies. 'You know what I mean, a notion for a woman, you know, a bit of the quare fellow!'

Tom the Saint's face was a study in emotions. 'Enough,' he says. 'You, sir, are beyond redemption. My mind dwells on higher things than the pleasures of the flesh. I leave that to you and your ilk. Your attitude to the word of the Lord is well known. Your behaviour, with your curly-headed whore in the village is well mapped-out, your sins will not be hidden from the Lord.'

" Covered only with a sack, he spent those killer
nights praying for forgiveness.... "

The Clareman has now succeeded in achieving his aim of vexing Tom, and is obviously enjoying himself. Lest he go too far, and drive the Saint into a rage, where he might run the Clareman through with a pitchfork, I shout at them. 'Will ye come on and throw up the hay, or are ye going to stay gabbing all day?'

Tom throws his arms wide and looks up at the sky. 'Out of the mouthes of babes,' he cried. 'Hark you, sinner, to the voice of the wise.'

He had been aptly named, our Tom the Saint. He was the copybook image of what our minds were conditioned to imagine a good class of saint should look like. He had never taken a razor in his hands. Since his early youth, when this religious mania first caught him in its grip, and the youthful down began to sprout on his cheeks, he had taken careful pattern of a character in a painting of the Stations of the Cross that adorned the walls of the Chapel. From then on, he used his scissors to shape his beard and the hair on his head to the model of his chosen idol. It seemed to have escaped his notice that the character he had chosen to emulate was in the process of kissing another tall saintly-looking man that a group of uncouth-looking ruffians were busily binding with ropes. . .

Tom was the scourge of parish priests and curates alike. He gloried in dramatics. He usually entered the church when the congregation was in its place, and Mass was about to begin. He walked in a slow shuffling gait with hands outstretched, until he reached the high altar, where the priest was about to commence the prayers before Mass, and then, uttering a loud moan, he stretched his full length on the floor, his face to the ground, uttering weird incantations. As his moans and groans began to die away, and the unfortunate priest began to hope he might be able to carry on with his business, Tom jumped up and moved to the women's aisle, where he again stretched his full length on the floor. This second move didn't seem to have any more significance than the first, except, as I suspected, to satisfy his sense of showmanship.

Tom now goes to his chosen seat and sits down. The priest turns his eyes towards Heaven, as if appealing to the Most High for assistance; if He could see His way to strike Tom the Saint dead in his tracks or, if He could not be that extreme, could He at least stick him to his seat for the duration of the Mass?

Tom, sensing that the excitement of his entrance and subsequent acrobatics is beginning to fade, jumps to his feet, turns his eyes to the ceiling, and with arms outstretched, utters a loud moan, followed by what sounds like the coo-ing of a hen, when she's about to lay an egg.

At this stage of his existence, Tom is an old man, probably in his mid-seventies. How he has survived to this age is a mystery, as the suffering he had inflicted on his body was unbelievable. The suffering he had inflicted on his brother and sister with whom he lived, was also unbelievable. His brother was the pilot for the River Deel – a waterway that would test the skill of any boatman. He maintained that when God made the Deel He'd had a 'drop taken', as its meanderings, on its journey to join the Shannon, left many a ship's captain scratching his head in amazement, as he watched his ship tacking and turning in pursuit of the elusive channel.

The pilot had been taking his brother Tom as a crewman in his rowing boat, when he was obliged to board one of these 'coasters' at the river mouth, and he now believed that from sheer repetition Tom was as capable of performing this task as himself. And so, one bleak and dark January morning, when the pilot was suffering from a streaming cold, and the after-effects of an over-abundance of porter the previous night, he was persuaded by his sister, 'against his better judgement', to allow Tom to journey on his own to the river mouth, and act as pilot for that occasion.

It was a day he would never forget, or be allowed to forget. The Deel, in spite of its twisting channel, was not marked by buoys, or indeed any type of warning markers. A pilot or a boatman depended on his skill at picking out landmarks. This was merely the lining-up of, perhaps, the chimney of a house with a bush growing in a field, or the pier of a gate with a rock on the shore. It was a system used for centuries by boatmen, and was in fact quite effective.

On the day of our story, Tom the Saint boarded the coaster off the great rock of Carrig Eire Vaun. She was loaded with coal. He entered the River Deel without effort, and proceeded along the channel towards the village. If he had a lapse of concentration, or merely became bored with the whole process, which he was quite capable of doing, the ship reached an area of the river known as the 'bangle'. As one may guess, it wasn't given this name for nothing.

The captain, standing on the bridge beside the Saint, noticed the reeds and rice grass growing along the river-bank begin to appear dangerously close to his ship. He turned to the 'pilot'. 'This seems a damnably dangerous waterway, is everything under control?'

'Fear not,' he said. 'The Lord is nigh. He shall deliver us from the roar of the tempest and the shoal water.'

The captain gave an uneasy look at his pilot, and an odd feeling came over him. He was a native of Liverpool, and had always felt that the Irish were an odd lot. The danger of his predicament had not yet struck him. He looked again at the pilot, he seemed interested in something far out in space. He was holding his head in that strange saintly position we have come to accept as the norm, the head turned down, but the eyes rolled upwards as far as possible in their sockets. Suddenly the ship lurched to port, and then spun violently to starboard as her keel ploughed through the mud along the channel's edge. She tore on, and eventually came to rest, almost literally in a farmer's yard.

For a moment the captain was speechless. Then he began jumping up and down, tears of frustration and rage streaming down his face. He grabbed his hair in fistfuls and attempted to pull it out by the roots. 'What will I do at all?' he shouted. 'What will I do at all? My ship is ruined, my ship is ruined.' He turned savagely on Tom. 'I knew it,' he said, 'I knew it the minute you came on board, you're mad, quite mad, you've more fucking hair on you than a fucking golly-wog. Who told you you were a pilot? Jesus Mary and Joseph, what will I do?'

Tom the Saint was standing away from the captain on the sloping deck of the bridge. 'I turn my face to you for your spittle,' he said. 'I hold my beard for your nails to tear, welcome be the will of the Lord.'

The captain began to move like a cat towards the pilot, his arms stretched before him, fingers bent as if in search of a neck to wring. In spite of his assertion to the contrary, the Saint decided that discretion was the better part of valour, and he began to retreat towards the bow of the ship. The vessel was wedged firmly in the mudbank, and had in fact had a miraculous escape, as it was aground between two notorious areas of rocks and foul ground. Tom scrambled over the bow and down the anchor chain, and when he reached the water, began to wade ashore.

The captain's face appeared over the railing. 'Come back,' he shouted. 'Come back! What am I going to do?'

Tom didn't turn, but over his shoulder he made a very unsaintly remark. 'Go shit,' he said. 'There she's for you, and you can take her or leave her.'

Three weeks later, after back-breaking work with picks and shovels during low tides, the ship was refloated and taken to the village and offloaded, none the worse for her experience. During her stay, Tom took great precautions to stay out of the firing line of the captain.

Overhead the river on the cliff top, and still standing to this day, is the whitethorn bush known to locals as 'Tom the Saint's Bush'. It was here he spent the nights when man or beast should not be outdoors. Only the nights of howling wind and rain would find him here. Bone-breaking frost and thunderstorms were to him as strong liquor to an alcoholic. Covered only with a sack, he spent those killer nights, praying for forgiveness for his own and others' sins. The fine nights he stayed indoors, to the utter consternation of his brother and sister. A huge Christmas candle would be lighted and put standing on the floor. He knelt beside it in a bolt-upright position, praying continually in a loud voice until the candle burned out. The appeals and curses of his brother and sister to have him 'put out the light and go to bed' fell on deaf ears. Tom's droning voice continued throughout the night and into daylight, until finally the candle burned out.

Tom's life, like that of the candle, also finally burned out. He had outlived his brother and sister by several years, and towards the end of his days seemed to increase the torture of his body. He was found sitting on his little sugain chair in the kitchen of his humble home, and was believed to have been dead for several weeks. During a search of the house to ascertain his financial position, two pennies were found under a saucer on the dresser.

It is said, we take into the next world only the good works we perform in this one. Tom probably never had the opportunity of performing many good works, but he was a harmless inoffensive creature. Who among us is to say he was not the stuff saints are made of . . .

The death of Tom the Saint seemed a watershed. Suddenly all the great characters of the village and parish began to fade away. Old Rooney was laid to rest, followed by my father, the beloved Pad, the one that loved me best of all. The great packs of duck and geese are no more to be seen on the mudbanks of the Shannon and Deel Estuaries. The all-out drive for material things has taken its toll on the Irish character. Perhaps Tom the Saint, quite unintentionally, left under the saucer on his dresser, a message for all of us. . .